Enjoy !

Betty &
Sümter
2010

THEY FAITHFULLY LED THE WAY

Remembering those who came before and helped create

WARREN WILSON COLLEGE

To Dick and Margi, with good memories of your years with us, Truly, Bev

Frederick and Beverly Ohler

Copyright © 2010 Beverly Ohler

They Faithfully Led the Way

ISBN number: 978-1-59712-447-8

Printed in the United States of America by
Catawba Publishing Company

Order from
Catawba Publishing Company
(704) 717-8452
www.catawbapublishing.com

This book is dedicated to the memory of all the Warren Wilson people honored on these pages, with gratitude for their lives that so enriched our own and countless others.

Credits:

Cover photograph — William Mosher
Cover words — Lisa Ohler Denman
Poems — Billy Edd Wheeler
Additional remembrances:
    Larry Adamson
    Jack Allison, Class of '63
    Jonathan Bliss '86
    Christa Bridgman '76
    Maryam Daftari '63
    Reva Watson Dietrich '53
    Jewell Cardwell Field '56
    Christine Laporte Gardiner '86
    Terri Godfrey '70
    Barbara Hempleman
    Ben and Betty Holden
    Suellen Hudson
    Henry Jensen
    Dean Kahl
    John Koegel '69
    Ernst and Pat Laursen
    Virginia McKinley
    Bill and Käthe Mosher
    Betty Nelson '62
    Milton Ohlsen '63
    Henry "Sherfey" Randolph
    Jean Ritchie
    Sam Scoville
    John Showalter
    Betty Siviter
    Dennis and Kay Stockdale
    Steve Williams
    Marion Yeager '88

PEOPLE REMEMBERED and HONORED
who FAITHFULLY LED THE WAY

Arthur Bannerman
Lucile Bannerman
Henry Jensen
Thekla Jensen
Reuben Holden
Bernhard Laursen
Kathrine Laursen
Sam DeVries
Annette Schafer
John Connet
Dwight Vining
Leon Deschamps
May Deschamps
Elizabeth Martin
William Klein
Elizabeth Klein
Gordon Mahy
Helen Mahy
James McClure Clarke
Elspeth Clarke
Joan Beebe
Martha Ellison
Virginia Rath
Hugo Doob
Samuel Millar
William Penfound
Ellen Penfound
Howard Thomas
Ruth Thomas

John Abernethy
Herbert Fitton
Warren Wilson Hampe
Mickey McConnell
Al Roberts
Christina and Victor Eliassen
Marian and Cyrus Anderson
Elena Law

INTRODUCTION

Since my husband, Frederick Ohler, died in 2004, I have been intrigued by the huge folder in his filing cabinet marked, "Memorials." Some of the pages are now yellowing with age because they were written in the 1950s, at the beginning of his ministry. Reading through them is like looking at a history of Warren Wilson College. Most of the sustainers – not quite the founders, but the next generation that believed in its mission of education, carried it forth from farm school to college and enabled it to grow – all had a place in that folder. They were our mentors, our fathers and mothers who parented us in those early years of Fred's tenure at the college. For each unique, extraordinary person, at his or her memorial service, Fred wrote a eulogy or a prayer or both, capturing so personally each individual life. It was usually surprising to the families how very well he knew their loved one, conveying the essence of their personality with just the right words.

This is our heritage, part of a genealogy of Warren Wilson. For those of us who work and learn here, these people lived and gave their lives to this college and made it what it is today. They worked tirelessly, for so little. I never heard much complaining about that, because no one made much more than another, even the administration. They were people with a mission, who believed in this place and cared deeply for it with all of their being.

The alumni from those early years bear witness to this. They were the lucky beneficiaries of teachers and leaders who were truly service-oriented, people who lived to make the world a better place. They worked long hours on the campus, and in their "spare" time they went into the communities around us and used their talents in whatever way those abilities directed. Their hard work and dedica-

11

tion was balanced by a remarkable sense of joy. I remember all of them having an astonishing sense of humor. There was much teasing and funny antics and great mirth. The campus was a cheerful place to be.

I have long thought that someday I would compose these memorials into a book to share with those who loved these people as we did, who learned from them and treasured them. I hope those new to the college will meet them too, and realize from whom we emerged.

Warren Wilson has always been a unique place, marching to its own drummer, trying to be true to the best way to learn and discover truth, special to each individual. Of course, not everyone who contributed significantly to the college is in this collection, but many are honored on these pages. This is not meant to be a history, just personal recollections of people we knew, some very well.

I have used Fred's words as the nucleus of this book, in some cases adding pertinent information. These were my friends too; I could not resist adding some of my memories. Everything in *italics* is my addition, usually beginning the chapter. In some cases I have included stories that others have written, and several Warren Wilson family members have graciously shared their poignant remembrances for this book. In every case they are given credit at the beginning of the piece, and their names appear in bold type.

I am grateful to Diana Sanderson in the WWC Archives for her kind help in finding pictures; to Lisa Ohler Denman for her expert help in editing and putting the book together; to Christa Bridgman, Terri Godfrey, Chrisann Ohler and everyone who encouraged me to publish it. Special appreciation to Jack Allison, Betty Nelson, Milton Ohlsen, and all the other contributors for remembering so well their years at Warren Wilson and the people who helped inspire their lives.

Beverly Ohler

ARTHUR BANNERMAN

DR. ARTHUR BANNERMAN was president of the college when we arrived. He was the reason we came to Warren Wilson after he journeyed up to Yale Divinity School looking for an intern for the religion department of Warren Wilson College just at the same time Fred was looking for an internship. He was a small man, large in spirit and intelligence who along with Henry Jensen, was most responsible for the success of the college.

He arrived in Swannanoa in 1928, interrupting his law studies in New Jersey to teach for a "little" while. He was born in Alaska to Presbyterian missionary parents, so likely he knew about the needs in National Missions from them. The Farm School was begun and supported by the Board of National Missions of the Presbyterian Church. His subject was history, and before becoming an administrator he taught classes, found and fell in love with his dearest Lucile just down the road, and stayed for the rest of his life.

He and Dr. Jensen, dean of the college, were the ying and yang of the campus, a perfect balance of talents and abilities. He was an excellent president, a gentle peacemaker who believed in shared governance. Everyone who worked on the campus had an equal voice — from the woman who ran the laundry to the Ph.D.s in the classroom. Respected and influential in the Presbyterian Church, Dr. B. took our college from a mission station of the church, to a junior college, to a full-fledged respected four-year institution. A skyscraper named for him would not be large enough to honor this man. He traveled widely to make our story known though out the country and around the world. In times of crisis, he had a wise and patient reaction and often came

13

up with just the right solution. Integrating a college in the South was not an easy thing to accomplish in 1952, but under Dr. B's leadership, it was done.

If you looked closely, his eyes sparkled mischievously. Each year at Christmas he was the funniest Santa to behold. We made him king in the Elizabethan Festival – our very own "King Arthur," and he wore his tights regally. When he retired, as part of the Appalachian Festival, we had a grand banquet in his honor and celebrated his life in words, film and song in a daisy-filled Gladfelter. A beloved and honored leader, he served the college so remarkably well for over forty years.

AT ARTHUR BANNERMAN'S MEMORIAL SERVICE IN 1976, FRED SPOKE THESE WORDS:

Little did I know that day in New Haven in 1955 when I first met Arthur Bannerman that my life would be changed – unalterably and forever and for the better.
How could I possibly have known that in the disguise of that quiet, spare, modest man
I had in fact met – King Arthur
      and begun my journey to Camelot?

He remained over the years – constant
      always there
      when others cut and ran
      when it was easy and when it was not.
A man for ALL seasons.
Often poor in things, always rich in soul
fair   faithful   whole.
What he said matched who he was,
and what he dreamed,
always demanding more of himself than he asked of others.

He had his fears and his shyness,
but he conquered them in private, lonely struggles –

giving us in this community and this college
his optimism
his historical perspective, his faith in Christ and Christ's Church.

Constant – and constantly surprising us
    with a twinkle in his eye
    with a smile on his lips
    with a long sigh in the midst of a long meeting
        that told us all (without a word spoken)
        that it was time to decide
        with the skinniest, jolliest and most loving Santa
        Claus we children ever saw.
Administrators and persons in authority are expected to be
    arrogant, assuming, in love with power.
What they should be
what they sometimes are – praise God – what Arthur Bannerman was:
    a man, strong but modest,
    a reconciler, a maker of peace,
    allowing, encouraging others to be and grow and fly –
knowing, because he was a Christian, that the greatest power in the world is the uncoercive, gentle force of love.

Dr. Jensen spoke of Arthur Bannerman so honestly: "His faith in people and his optimism in the midst of difficulties have provided steadiness and confidence in many critical periods. His insistence upon participation by all who are concerned and willingness to accept responsibility have kept a climate in which students and staff could find an ever-widening share of governance. He was ever ready to delegate authority and permit experimentation by those who are ready to live with the results... Night and day, day and night for a lifetime, Warren Wilson has been Arthur Bannerman's labor of love."

Years of grace – a final year of grace – and we are grateful.

They Faithfully Led the Way

Perhaps Billy Edd speaks for many of us in these words:

DADDY B.
(1900-1976)

Of all the fathers
I have searched for in this world,
you were the best
        including blood kin
        adopted kin, spiritual dads
        and mental. You were fun
        to be with, lofty, loving,
        elemental.

You rounded out my world.

You drew out of me
poems and cusswords
I never knew I had, especially poems.

You were my buddy
        and my adversary.
        We warren on the golf course,
        pool table, athletic field
        living room and telephone.

You outstroked me
outwalked me
outshot me outbet me
outpsyched me.
But I made you cuss, too
        you crusty old scrapper.
        Though damn it was mostly
        all that came out. Your eyes
        let me know where I stood.
        They cussed a-plenty.

And that was good. (Sometimes
sons and would-be poets take too
much unpoetic license).

You taught me how to win
    with humility
    and lose with honor.

You were so good with people.
You loved them.
You knew their families
clear back to great-great
    and who married who.
You were so good for me to measure
    against and stand next to.
You were the largest man
in the smallest body I ever knew.
You were Craggy Mountain
in the softness of Dogwood Ridge.
You were the general
in the cap and smile of a private.
You were Mr. President
in the care and concern of a missionary.

You rounded out my world.
And just as much as you gave me you
you gave me me.

Thank you, Mr. President.
That you, Craggy, General,
Buddy, Opponent, Friend.
Thank you Daddy B.

Billy Edd Wheeler,
son-in-law, alumnus,
poet, composer, lyricist, artist

A few years ago, in 2005, **Barbara Hempleman** *(WWC teacher, librarian, archivist) wrote an insightful piece about Dr. Bannerman. It not only tells a lot about this remarkable man, but also about the college as it was in earlier years. With her permission I've copied most of it here:*

"When I came to the campus in 1948, he and his daughter Mary met me at the train station in Swannanoa – my introduction to this remarkable but modest man. They lived in a log cabin that the college had bought from Miss Elizabeth Williams. The Bannermans had lived for a time in Randolph Hall, built by students for Dr. Randolph when he had been head of the school. He had eight children. The Bannerman family was smaller, so they gave up Randolph to be used by students and later for faculty housing.

I knew Dr. Bannerman as president of Warren Wilson College during the years that I taught history at the college, and when I lived on campus as a faculty wife. I also had the opportunity as college archivist to read correspondence, memos, minutes of meetings and other records which told about the more than 30 years that he headed the school.

In addition to being president, Dr. Bannerman taught a college sociology course and co-sponsored the international relations club for several years. When allowed by the Board of National Missions of the Presbyterian Church in the USA to go out and raise money for the college, Dr. Bannerman excelled at fund raising, gaining contributions from churches, individuals and foundations. During his presidency the school grew from a boys' high school to a coeducational junior college and then to a four-year college accredited by the Southern Association of Schools and Colleges. He worked with the Board to promote and coordinate these changes. Also as president he planned for and oversaw the construction of many buildings: Sage, Stephenson, Dorland, Schafer Court, and Vining dormitories, Morse Science Hall, Spidel, Ellison Library, Bannerman Lecture Hall, Ogg Administration Building, Gladfelter, the

College Chapel, DeVries Gymnasium, Shepard House, the Boiler Room, and at least 20 faculty houses.

In the 1940s and 50s, he worked on integration on the campus and in the community. This included annual meetings of the Hazen Conference which was an interracial meeting of college administrators and religious leaders. He did this quietly, as that was his manner and also so that there would not be any more negative repercussions on the college than absolutely necessary. As the college made changes – ballroom dancing and integrated conferences on campus, the admission of Japanese students during World War II, German, Dutch and Czechoslovakian students soon after the war, then African-American, Arab, Iranian, Greek, Chinese and Korean students in the 1950s – the college continued to be respected and appreciated by people in Western North Carolina.

Dr. Bannerman was the person who reached out to participate in and be the face of Warren Wilson in the surrounding community. He smiled, was courteous, and continued to encourage and cause radical changes to happen on the campus as being good for the college, with the hope that some of Warren Wilson's ways would cause positive changes in the world around us. He also gave personal time and thought helping individual students who came from rural homes with no money for education and barely enough of life's necessities. He talked graciously with people from Biltmore Forest and with naïve young staff members. I remember a conversation with him in 1949 regarding how many communists we could have on the staff without it being a problem. He was undoubtedly chuckling inside at how little I knew about the world but was enjoying the play of ideas and certainly was not bothered by differences of opinion.

For many years he chaired faculty meetings. This included discussion of matters of concern to teachers and to work supervisors and, on the principle that all of us were teaching students in class or work, "faculty" included all the staff, meeting and voting together on the operation of the school. All students worked a twenty-hour week until the federal work-study program shortened the hours. The maintenance of the college was done by students with a staff supervisor for each crew, and work was a learning experience as well as a way to keep the place running. Thus, when a vote was taken in staff meeting, the senior teacher in the English or math department had a vote equal to that of the college nurse, the secretary, the person in charge of plumbing and heating, the farmer and the house mother. I was young and inexperienced so took this as commonplace rather than as the unusual system that it was.

I also accepted as a matter of fact that we all had our say in staff meetings, regardless of whether we agreed or disagreed with the administration or with the Board of National Missions in New York, who really owned the school. It seemed perfectly normal and good that after having our say in a sometimes lively way with Dean Jensen, who was very influential – often one of the last to speak, Dr. Bannerman had us vote on an issue so that a conclusion was reached. We didn't all always agree with the conclusion and the action that it would call for, but we were able to keep our grumbling to a minimum and carry out the decision or, at least, to live with it.

Having worked in other places and for other presidents and deans, I have come to realize what an exceptional skill Dr. Bannerman had with his ability to chair such open meetings in which we all discussed, could disagree, and then he somehow pulled us together to vote, making and accepting a decision that kept the school operating in a positive way. There were times when he delayed decision making and people fussed about the delay, but this was often a deliberate delay, as Dr. Bannerman knew that people weren't ready to make a decision that would enable plans to go forward. He could stand in his office or sit at his desk and pass a paper from one hand to the next and look indecisive. He could sit at staff meeting and cross one leg over the other and then reverse the process while the staff debated at length until a good solution to a problem evolved or was recognized. Then he could reach out into the group and call on the right person or appoint the right person to a committee to get a decision made or a task taken care of. I see this as a quiet genius at work in administration.

I watched this in a meeting when the staff was debating whether or not to graduate a high school senior who committed the error of getting drunk the last week of school, obviously breaking a serious rule. There were strong feelings expressed on both sides: those who thought that boys will be boys, and those who certainly were not going to let him out with a Warren Wilson diploma. A silence fell with various staff members seated, arms crossed on their chests in a determined way. Then he called on Miss Eila Carson, housemother of the only dormitory for boys, 'Miss Eila, you haven't spoken and you must know him quite well.' Miss Eila, whose chair was tipped back against the logs in the old library where the meeting was held, brought all legs down on the floor and said, 'I would be happy to see him graduated.' In a moment nearly everyone laughed, realizing that she would be happy to have him move on out of her dormitory. As the mood had changed, Dr. Bannerman asked if we were ready to vote. We were and we graduated him.

Dr. Bannerman, as college president, moved the college in ways that are still admired and considered radical by many people, ways that moved toward the social justice ideals of Christianity and the open inclusive ideals of today's youth. He did this in a manner that was very low key. As a result, we all knew that we were very active participants in the process, which encouraged us to work hard for these results and to do our job, and the surrounding community did not feel threatened by our radical ideas.

I do not remember him ever talking about his religious convictions, but they were visible in his actions. He made big commitments to social justice and to internationalism at the college. He was willing to take risks for a world committed to equality, openness, and to a global concept of loving our neighbors."

Speaking of loving our neighbors, on a global AND a more local level, alumna, rehabilitation counselor and former trustee **Betty Nelson** *shares this story about Dr. B:*

"When I was a student, the Ohlers lived in Preston across from the president's house. My first Christmas, both Ani Wong Lelea and I stayed on campus for the holiday break. The Ohlers were headed to New Jersey for the holidays and were kind enough to let us stay in their home rather than the dorm while they were gone. Ani and I were thrilled one morning when we awoke to find everything covered in a beautiful snowfall, so pristine, clean and white. Ani was especially in awe as she had rarely seen snow in her San Francisco life.

We made some coffee and were sitting in the living room sipping our morning brew when we heard a knock on the door. We looked at each other with surprise wondering who would be out in this weather. Upon answering the door, we discovered Dr. B standing there with a snow shovel over his shoulder, saying he was just 'checking on' us 'girls' to be sure we were okay in this cold snowy weather! He had shoveled all the way down his driveway, across the road and up the long driveway just to check on us. Sure never heard of a college president anywhere else doing that. He was such a dear man."

Alumna and diplomat-sinologist **Maryam Daftari**, *then a student from Iran, recalls him this way:*

"I remember Dr. Bannerman very fondly. It was my first year in college, and I was lonely at first. Dr. Bannerman made me feel important and loved by taking me to meetings of the Lions, Kiwanis and Rotary Clubs. He would ask me to talk about Iran — the political, economic, social and cultural aspects. I loved to do that, for I felt I was telling people things that they did not know. It gave me great satisfaction, and I felt I was doing a service. Thus I accompanied him on several of such trips every semester.

I came to love his sense of humor, his pleasant demeanor and his intelligence. Wonderful memories stand out for me of WWC because of him."

Arthur Bannerman

LUCILE BANNERMAN

THE FOLLOWING WERE FRED'S WORDS AT HER MEMORIAL SERVICE IN 1996:

It was the year before my last year at Yale Divinity School. Bev and I were 23 and fresh from our honeymoon when we arrived on the campus of Warren Wilson... green, untried, intern Yankee missionaries. We were instantly greeted and warmly welcomed by every one, but especially by the president's wife. From the very moment we met, Lucile Bannerman was gracious and loving and respectful. She never ever caused us to feel inadequate or unable; she was "all ways" encouraging and supportive. Thus began a relationship, a deep friendship that has lasted over forty years.

Honoring all she gave, celebrating all she was, let us pray:

Lord, we recall that Lucile never feared silence, that she loved to listen, that she could communicate without a word spoken. We approach YOU first in silent prayer, remembering... seeing... appreciating Lucile...

She was, in the truest and deepest sense, a Christian, a teacher, an artist (her touch transformed a log bungalow into her man's castle and every guest's hearth of home; her inspiration kept the arts alive at Warren Wilson; she was instrumental in the building of this beautiful chapel). She was always the gracious and enabling hostess, worrying the details into perfection, shy of accolades or attention, making Eleanor Roosevelt or the newest freshman feel equally well come. As a sister, a wife, a mother, a mother-in-law, a grandmother, her work was her vocation was her love.

Like Thoreau at Walden, she stayed mostly at home, never wandering too far for very long from her beloved Swannanoa Valley, which has been "the place just right" for her family for more than two centuries. And, like Thoreau, she was the least provincial of persons. Lord, You sent the world to her valley and to her heart and she welcomed Your revelations in. How she mothered our first international students, learned from outlanders and added new colors to her palette while always being proudly Appalachian, and keeping us all rooted in this "valley of love and delight," beauty and grace, where You so stunningly set us.

Thank You, God, that in Lucile You gave us the impeccable eye of an artist, the patience of a teacher, the strength of a mountain woman, the bearing of nobility. We celebrate her taste, her love of everything natural, subtle, wood, green, her regal carriage, dignity and integrity, her profound, subtle, pervasive influence on this college, on this entire community.

We pray Your presence, Your reality with us all, but especially with Lucile's sisters, her brother, and with Janet, Mary, Billy Edd, Lucy and Travis. They've had time to get ready for her leaving; who is _ever_ ready? Almost a year ago, Lucile came back from the dead, having seen her true love and Heaven, and she was ready. But we needed more time and You granted it, that we might become reconciled to her leaving. God, help _us_ to be ready-for death and life and loving... through Christ our Lord, Amen.

* * * * *

The following is from a 1996 remembrance written by **Ben Holden:**

"Lucile Patton Bannerman spent her entire life in this valley. Many of us pass the house every day where she was born in 1910, just two miles down the road. The Pattons were one of the oldest and best known families in this part of the state. She went to our sister school, Asheville Normal and Teachers College, and then taught at the Swannanoa Elementary School. No one knew more about this area, and she was rightly proud of her heritage.

Lucile had a mind of her own and spoke her piece when called for. She did not like to hear 'patronizing' the Farm School as a place for poor or underprivileged students. It was a school that had a farm where students proudly learned to work and appreciate a full academic program.

Her 45 years as the wife of Arthur Bannerman were happy ones for them, as indeed they were for the college community. Her hospitality, charm, warmth and great thoughtfulness endeared her to all. She was a friend and mentor to many students who loved her dearly.

Although she rarely traveled a great deal, she said the world had come to her in this valley, where she developed a passionate love of beauty, both in nature and in art. The history of this place was written in her bones. Her mind was curious and explorative. She wanted students and staff to have as much exposure to as much art as possible, sponsoring exhibits in Gladfelter and talks by artists. She educated her eye on college trips to New York and Washington. Painting became a way of life for her. She began to see art in everything – the way people decorated their homes, what they chose to wear, how they combined colors.

A kind person, she would regularly write notes to those she felt deserved praise or encouragement. She called me often at 8 a.m. to comment on campus events or problems, joys or worries she had during the night. Warren Wilson and her family were her whole life. She never failed to keep track about what was happening on the campus. The smallest detail was important.

She never lacked humor. Shortly after I took office here, I called to see if I could make a late afternoon call on Lucile and Art; I needed comfort and advice on some critical matter. When I arrived at the door, they took one look at me and said, 'Ben, you look like you need a strong shot of bourbon!' At the Orthopedic Hospital she said she was beginning to be known as the most difficult patient there; she told the nurses blankly what she would and wouldn't do. Finally, she said in the most genial way, 'Well, I guess it's time to call Dr. Kevorkian!'

As her eyes began to fail more and more, her ears became more acute – and she really saw everything. She recognized voices and forms. Brave and strong of spirit, her inner radiance in this past year of suffering shone forth with radiance. It doesn't matter how old you are, it is a matter of how you are old."

Lucile Bannerman

HENRY JENSEN

Dr. HENRY JENSEN was lovingly called "DOC" by almost everyone. It was his philosophy of education that helped perpetuate the dream of what the college became.

He was educated at Harvard and had a decidedly Boston accent. His Ph.D. in botany served him well when he helped design and landscape the campus. When we first came to Warren Wilson, he was the college dean, the director of the work program, the head of the landscaping crew (called "The Landscratchers") and a respected professor of botany.

He wrote a personal letter to every student who ever applied to the school, whether or not they were accepted. The longest letters were sometimes written to those who did not qualify to be admitted. He always tried to direct students on their right path to a successful future.

Doc had very poor eyesight and wore thick glasses that gave him an owl-like appearance, but on his botany hikes through the campus, students could hardly keep up with him, taking notes as he pointed out the species he had planted throughout the 1000 acres that is Warren Wilson.

Alum and WWC registrar **Christa Bridgman** *was Doc's last student secretary. He always managed to have the most capable and efficient help through the years, especially important because of his eyesight, and every one of his secretaries was devoted to him. Christa typed the history of Warren Wilson that he and Bidge Martin had written together. When Doc retired, Christa sculpted his likeness in clay as a special tribute to her beloved boss.*

Each year at the assembly, an annual event the week before students left for Christmas break, the entire community would gather to listen to one of Doc's original Christmas stories. Selections of them were published in two editions, THE LITTLE SEEDS OF CHRISTMAS (1964) and TALES FROM CHRISTMAS RIDGE (1973). In the foreword/dedication of the latter, Doc wrote: "These tales were prepared for a very special audience which was enjoying an exceedingly special season. Here the concern is with the Spirit of Christmas and its often surprising manifestation among people of the twentieth century who possess sufficient sensitivity to be moved by its presence. Among that company are a host of Warren Wilson College faculty, staff, alumni and students, to whom this volume is affectionately dedicated."

Doc accompanied himself on the guitar as he sang his original songs at many college functions. An album called BROOM SEDGE BAL- LADS records him singing and accompanying his tunes. The WWC alma mater, which Doc wrote and composed, is considered by many the best they've ever heard. His guitar is currently displayed with other artifacts in a beautiful case in Jensen, the building named for him on campus. Inspired by the beauty which surrounded him, occasionally he would also set up his easel and paint.

A greatly respected, talented leader, Henry Jensen spent more than forty years creatively working and developing our college.

FRED'S WORDS FROM HENRY JENSEN'S SERVICE IN 1975:

OPENING PRAYER:

O God, Henry has died – and when a giant dies there is such loss,
such an absence that we can't believe it.
We, his friends and neighbors, remember him with gratitude
for all he did and thought, dreamed and was
year in and year out –
when it was easy and when it wasn't.

Receive the special memory and prayer of each of us
as we reach out together in silence.
Help us never forget his faith,
his conviction about Your providence,
his perception of Your grace.

WORDS OF REMEMBRANCE:

"To bind together… as long as I sing…"
Henry can no longer sing,
and I can almost imagine him saying last week
in that clear, good New England voice,
"Wouldn't you like to leave it all behind sometime?
All is still – go to sleep my restless soul
I'm tired of having to stay where night is just day after day,
And when I am weary of watching the sky
I'd set down well westward to die…"

Henry can no longer sing,
but we cannot ever forget his song –
the song of a free man
who journeyed a long way   from Eden to Denmark
to Boston   to the Swannanoa Valley,
who found his place – just right   in this place
            In this valley.

Henry was a complex man – many men in one man,
a magnificent teacher – brilliant enough to master his specialty,
too wise to be limited to it,
and so generations of students learned
in the field – in the office – in the chapel – in the classroom,
botany, philosophy, theology, poetry – life.
An artist with brush and voice and words.
A scientist – like Loren Eiseley or Chardin,
whose critical perceptive, disciplined hunger for truth

laughed at narrow limits,
and whether he peered at a violet or gazed into the heavens,
he did so with vigor and doubt of half-truths and good faith.

He was a complex man – liberal and conservative,
an embodiment of Tennyson's
"There is more faith in honest doubt than in half the creeds."
AND a profoundly religious man.
Long before I ever read Chardin, he excited my mind
in a long discussion of God as changing, evolving – beyond our
imagining.
This same man spoke of the Lord – sincerely and openly,
sensitive and aware of other religions,
and a committed Christian.
Totally practical, he was also, though he denied it more than
once,
a mystic.
He had little patience with humbug;
he could spot shame at a thousand yards.
He would weary with the words of little men,
and he did not heed man's empty praise.
Long before theologians spoke about and wrote books about the
theology of hope,
Henry hoped hugely,
and had such vision,
and dreamed great dreams.
He was usually a generation ahead of the rest of us,
and his dreams, more often than not, came true in this place,
and in our lives.
He was a gifted administrator,
and he had such courage to take the unpopular stand,
to consider very carefully and then to decide,
and then, like a man, take his stand responsibly.

No man better understood the providence of God,
for so much good came to him in a woman who loved him

with a great and beautiful love.
In all his friends, his children (i.e. his students), his works –
no man better understood the grace of God,
for Henry never presumed on God, but graciously received and spent
God's lavish gifts upon him.

Henry was a complex man –
but he was also simple, as Thoreau was simple.
He found the simple gift of cutting away the dross
and focusing on what was essential.

Henry and I did not always agree,
and once we hurt each other deeply,
but he was the only genius I ever met.
I've saved every letter he ever wrote me.
One of them came just after writing the history of Warren Wilson.
It is one of my dearest treasures.

He was a great, good man who meant more to me than I think he ever knew.
Other than my father, he was the most important man in my life.

* * * * *

Betty Nelson *has told the following story many times, for good reason. It tells clearly what Doc was like and just what kind of a school it was in 1960:*

"When I arrived on campus in September 1960, I was a very naïve 17 year old from Michigan. No one in my family had ever gone to college before, we did not have much money, and I had no idea what the cost for college would be, having never even seen the current college catalogue.

After high school graduation in June, I had worked in a factory to save money for college, but at $1.05/hour, not much was saved after paying rent and buying some college clothes. What I did have, though, I withdrew from the bank and bought a Greyhound bus ticket to Asheville, then paid for a taxi from the bus depot to campus; the remainder of my money I took to Carson Hall, found Doc's office and told his student worker I needed to see Doc.

Doc invited me into his office, and I announced I was there to pay my fees. He replied, 'That's a fine way to start your college career.' I asked how much the fees were. He said, 'How much do you have?' I pulled myself up to my full five-foot-three-inch height and said, '$75.' Doc looked me straight in the eye and said, 'That's exactly what it costs!' He put out his hand; I handed him all my money. And that was the last I heard from him, or anyone else, about college fees for my two years at Warren Wilson Junior College.

I was never once made to feel I had not paid my own way. In fact I never gave it another thought… until I was ready to transfer to Berea College for the final 2 years of my BA, and Doc assisted me to obtain some Presbyterian Home Missions grants and loans to pay Berea. The thought struck me then that I had not paid much to WWC, but Doc never raised the issue, and I was too busy with graduation and transferring to give it much real consideration. The thought occurred to me again when I graduated from Berea and applied for a federal grant to pay for graduate school at University of Kentucky. But again it was just a passing thought. Upon graduating from UK, I moved to California and began my 35-year career as a rehabilitation counselor, later moving to Oregon where I eventually opened a private practice, rehabilitation counseling & consulting firm.

It was not until 1984 when I returned to WWC for a visit that I decided to find out the truth about my college fees… so I asked student records to let me see my old file. I sat down and started reading the file and was dumbfounded to see letter after letter from Doc to people he knew around this country, asking them to contribute money to help this needy student meet her college expenses! I really had no idea. And people were generous, so generous, and I thank God they were, because I could never have paid for the excellent education I received at WWC. And that is one reason I contribute each year to the college now as an alumna... in hopes that it will help another needy student (though I suspect that today there aren't any quite as naïve as I was)."

Some additional remarks from **Betty Nelson** *about Doc:*

"Dr. Jensen was a Renaissance man. I personally found him to be a joy to talk with and share stories; I enjoyed getting to know him. I met that fun side of him, but he also had high expectations of people and could be a stern disciplinarian as dean of the college. Doc was an excellent teacher, and students loved his botany classes though they were very tough; he was not an easy grader and expected good work from each person.

In those days on campus, noon chapel was required twice per week – Tuesday and Thursday. It was called 'chapel' because that is where we met (in the old Williams' Chapel, recently torn down), though they were not necessarily religious meetings but rather a time to hear a visiting lecturer or for Doc to 'lecture' us about some problem or event we needed to tend to, or sometimes for him to sing his tunes. One lecture I remember especially was the one on the *Pinus strobus* (pine trees found just off the old coach road between the current chapel and the dorms on Sage Circle). Seems too many students were using the *Pinus strobus* as a necking and make out place after dark. Most anyone from that era can still name a *Pinus strobus* when we have forgotten the scientific names of all other trees!

In my opinion Doc was a great man – he made some unbelievably good decisions and he made a few not so good ones, but when he decided something he was willing to discuss why. He took a lot of flak sometimes because he ran this school in creative ways and WWC was always on the cutting edge educationally.

After I graduated, Doc and I carried on a correspondence for many years… amazing for a man as busy as he was. I learned from others that they, too, carried on a correspondence with him. If one wrote him they got an answer, usually typed by Doc himself."

Maryam Daftari *remembers Dr. Jensen with these words:*

"When I came to WWC from Iran, Dr. Jensen was one of the first professors I met. He welcomed me with great kindness and interest. We became close because of his (and my) interest in music. We performed several times together, he on his guitar, and me on the piano. He was also my botany professor, a truly great teacher. I had no interest in botany, but he stimulated my interest, and I came to love it.

He was a musician, a scientist, a great teacher, a writer, and a great humanist. He towered above all the rest, and above all, he had great humility. My father always said that the greatest test of a great man is his humility. Dr. Jensen was that great man."

Jewell Cardwell Field, *who was still a student during our internship year of 1955-56, writes this:*

"Early afternoon on a late 1954 August Saturday, I arrived with Dad at WWC. The campus was deserted. Unfamiliar with the WWC campus, or any college for that matter, Dad and I drove slowly along the narrow roads. Between what I was soon to learn were the chapel and the store, we came upon a man in gardener's clothes deftly using a pitchfork to move brush. He turned when Dad approached him. 'We're trying to find a building named Sage.'

Hair fell across his sweaty forehead. His eyes, behind his round thick glasses, seemed slightly crossed. 'Up this road, across the main highway, keep left to the end.' He returned to his pitch forking.

Imagine my surprise on Monday morning when I reported to the chapel for freshman orientation and was addressed by yesterday's ill-clad gardener —now in white shirt and tie.

Dr. Henry Jensen, as a botany teacher, filled my head with botanical facts and my soul with a reverence for plants. Dr. Jensen, as a dean, arranged a scholarship to cover my cash from pocket costs. Dr. Jensen, as Doc, had a profound influence on who I am today."

Henry Jensen

THEKLA REGINA JENSEN

Unfortunately, Thekla Jensen's memorial service was one of two missing from the file of the services that Fred conducted. I don't have his words, so I will try to tell her story.

Thekla came to the Farm School as Henry's young bride in 1933 shortly after they were married. I often try to imagine how she felt arriving from Boston, standing on that tiny train platform in Swannanoa. It was in the midst of the Great Depression and jobs were scarce even for someone with a Harvard Ph.D. It must have been quite an adjustment for this intelligent, cultured Danish woman. I think they were paid 32 dollars a month, but at least there was some housing and food.

She soon realized that Henry was a very good teacher and loved the classroom. They intended to stay one year, but it ended up being their home for the rest of their lives. She grew to be grateful that Henry had the opportunity to help the school grow into a college, a fine institution that needed her husband's wisdom.

When Doc became dean of the college Thekla, who was a gifted cook, assumed her role as hostess and entertainer. It was always such a pleasure for faculty and staff to be invited to the Jensen home for dinner. The table was always beautifully set with fine china and silver, and the food was mouth watering, with everything meticulously prepared. She brought a touch of European sophistication to the Swannanoa Valley.

Thekla was a voracious reader and had a sharp and intuitive mind. I'm sure she was a great help to Henry when there were difficult

43

matters to decide. They had a very strong marriage and loved each other dearly. After a difficult day, Henry always looked forward to his home and his love.

Alumnus, retired medical doctor, and relief volunteer **Jack Allison** *shares this about his friend:*

"I will call her Regina, because she preferred her middle name and that is what I called her. Regina was a quiet introvert who was totally devoted to her husband. She had lunch ready for Doc daily, so that he could have a brief respite from the rigors of being dean and chief operating officer of Warren Wilson. She was a fastidious housekeeper, and a marvelous cook who had one hard rule: 'Stay out of my kitchen!' Her Swedish meatballs were the very best.

In the early 1980s my wife, Sue, and I (along with our two little ones) invited Regina to join us on a picnic at Craggy Gardens on the Blue Ridge Parkway north of Asheville. When asked what she preferred for lunch, she replied enthusiastically, 'McDonald's!' That was indeed her favorite day-to-day restaurant. But, every time I visited Warren Wilson, be it for homecoming or for medical meetings nearby, Regina always graciously joined me for dinner at an upscale local restaurant. Those quiet, meaningful conversations remain in my marrow. Our son, Josh, was born on August 3, 1982. Sue and I honored Regina by naming him Joshua Jensen Allison. Doc had died seven years earlier.

Regina's frail body, then her perceptive mind gradually failed her. Her income was dwindling and I was asked to help her decide to sell her home and enter Highland Farms Retirement Community. Regina wanted to do neither. Although I was successful, I could see the profound disappointment in her loving eyes. Regina died shortly thereafter. I wept openly when I received word of Regina's death. She was the oldest friend that Sue and I had ever had who was just that − a dear, dear friend."

The following is a poem written about her by
Billy Edd Wheeler*:*

REGINA
(Mrs. Henry Jensen)

You gave me the perfect gift
in a book of poetry.
Back then ... when your face was attractive
and smooth and you were a line of verse.
I was touched.
Not only could I feast
on juicy word fruit
but save the seeds
to fill up and flower
barren orchards of my mind.
Your gift of kindness showed me
I had never written a poem.
Verses only.
Poem is a sacred word.
Now you give me another gift
a perfect gift
that touches me deeper than before.
My orchards bend
late blooming limbs
to greet the cooling breeze
your gift of love and promise.
You sit like Denmark's Queen
to full flowered garden
and hand me Doc's guitar
smiling through your sad eyes,
today ... when your face is beautiful
and wrinkled
and you are a poem.

Doc, Billy Edd Wheeler and Thekla

REUBEN ANDRUS HOLDEN

Dear Ben, dear, dear Ben. His name was Reuben, but to everybody he was Ben, our gentle Ben. There is not much to add to Fred's words about Ben because he says it all so well. He came to us after Dr. B. retired, and we had fifteen years of his leadership, though we needed more.

When Ben retired, we produced a festival in His honor – A FESTIVAL FOR BEN, and managed to truly surprise him. We wrote a play, a musical about his life which simultaneously traced what was happening on this campus while he was growing up. His daughter, Mary, brought his first grandchild from Paris, and he carried the baby onto the stage in Kittredge at the end of the play. As part of the festival, we had a banquet at the Grove Park Inn complete with string quartet and entertainment worthy of the honoree. Ben's brother, John, a California director, came to emcee the event to which everybody was invited. Ben never stopped smiling.

The Holden Art Building is named for Ben – person extraordinaire! I never met anyone who knew him who didn't love him. When he first came to the college, we were having a festival to celebrate childhood. Each year the festival had a different theme. The previous one had been the Elizabethan Festival with Dr. B. as king. This particular year we needed a storybook character for whom to celebrate a birthday with a huge campus-wide party, so we asked Dr. Holden who his favorite was. He replied, "Winnie the Pooh." So we planned a birthday party for Pooh. Unbeknownst to us, Ben went to NYC and rented THE Winnie the Pooh costume in which he dressed and came to the party dancing his little jig, hardly able to breathe in that giant Pooh head on a very hot day in Gladfelter. That's the kind of person he was.

His wife **Betty Holden** *reminds us of this wonderful side of Ben:*

"He immersed himself in humor of all kinds. He loved to laugh, sometimes uproariously. There was a T-shirt that he liked wearing on which was printed 'GLAD YOU MET ME.'

Ben would drive around campus with a musical car horn that son George had installed, playing 'Jingle Bells' or 'Happy Birthday' or 'La Cucaracha' or whatever he thought appropriate for the students he passed by. He would sometimes pick up the phone and answer, 'Macy's basement.' *(Note from Bev – Fred did the same thing, only he answered, 'City Morgue!')*

When Gracie returned home he would greet her, 'Welcome home, blithe spirit.'

Ben lived in lightness. Remember the book, 'THE UNBEAR-ABLE LIGHTNESS OF BEING?' That phrase reminds me of Ben's life."

How could one ever forget his funny though tasteful ties, especially the ones at Christmas that lit up or blinked. When he approached you he had the most hospitable smile that lit up his face. When we made him king of the Renaissance Festival, we thought he would be regal and majestic, but not Ben! Surrounded by his court of jesters, he was the silliest, tipsiest monarch, reigning over the banquets with fun and much frolic. Like Dr. Bannerman before him, he was such a perfect balance of capable efficiency and, as Betty described, "lightness of being."

Before coming to WWC, Ben had been secretary of Yale University, a much more important position than the title suggests. Years later we noticed it was Ben who signed Fred's diploma from Yale. He was second in line to the presidency, and when the powers-that-be made the terrible mistake of not advancing him, he found his own college, and we were the lucky recipients of his talents.

The college grew in many ways during Ben's time with us. We became much better known nationwide, he raised a good deal of needed money for growth, he strengthened the morale of the college, added programs and buildings, the MFA for writers, and, like Dr. Bannerman, brought many well-known people to the campus. He had so many friends, many in high places, including the President of the United States. When Ben retired, he left a campus of grateful and loving friends.

The gallery in Holden is named for Ben's wife, Betty, equally as dear a person as he was. She is a gifted poet and writer, a gracious, gentle, lovely woman, and a generous patron of the arts. She taught occasional courses in the English department, helped in all the festivals, was a kind and caring hostess to campus functions, and is a trusted friend to many. Betty still resides in Black Mountain, actively engaged in her many interests.

FROM THE MEMORIAL SERVICE FOR BEN HOLDEN AT THE WARREN WILSON PRESBYTERIAN CHURCH & COLLEGE CHAPEL, DECEMBER, 1995:

OPENING WORDS:

We are here – from around the campus,
from up the valley, from across the community
and all over the world,
because Ben Holden has died.
We are here because Ben Holden lived.
Oh, **how** he lived!
in Kentucky and Connecticut and China,
in Cincinnati and Krasnya Polyana
and Black Mountain.
We are here because Ben lived in God's world
and in our lives.

The public life and the private man were one;
he was as good in person as he was great in service.
Each of us thinks, "Ben was my special friend,
my **best** friend."
And all of us are right.
We are here because Ben loved every one of us (and thousands more)
by name, by heart.

We are here because "attention must be paid,"
sorrow divided and gratitude multiplied,
and our great respect truly expressed.
We are here to cry and to sing,
to pray and to remember,
to honor our friend and worship our God,
whose Love is All… **in** all.

INVOCATION:

Breathe… breathe slowly, breathe deeply.
Breathe, Holy Spirit, Breath of God,
into our bodies and souls,
into the depths of our doubts and the heights of our faith.
Enable, inspire us to find ourselves by getting lost…
lost in wonder, lost in love, lost in praise.
Wonder… at life and death and resurrection,
wonder at each breath and every miracle.
Lost in love…
which made Ben *Ben*, makes life possible,
liberates us from our sullen cells of ego to be our true selves
and touch each other's lives.
Lost in praise…
for every grace and each moment,
for life's sweetness and death's astringent clarity,
for… for Ben Holden's *Wonderful Life*

for Your extravagant Love...
through Christ our Lord
who lived   and died   and lives forever.

A PRAYER FOR BEN:

Lord, many of us prayed for a miracle,
knowing that only a miracle would do.
The miracle we got was not the one we asked for,
but miracle no less.
Thank You, God, for sparing Ben and his family and us all
months of suffering and endless pain.
But we didn't have time to adjust, to prepare...
most of all, to say, "Goodbye, old friend,"
though Ben surely would have been uncomfortable with that.

We remember and celebrate and marvel at all he did
and who he was… president, secretary, trustee, chairman,
war hero (though he'd be the last one to ever tell you that), educator, administrator, Presbyterian elder, exemplary Rotarian, citizen,
son, brother (closer than a twin to Johnny, whose dying hurt him
so)…   father (dear God, we're losing too many great fathers),
grandfather,
friend, human being.
He **was** "a prince among men,"
a man "too gentle to live among wolves," a Christian,
more of a minister than most who are ordained as such,
and the best chaplain Warren Wilson or Yale ever had.

When people sometimes hurt him
or took advantage of his good manners and gracious goodness,
he never paid back
or lashed out
or cut another down.
He came closer to living the Sermon on the Mount

than most of us ever dream or *imagine*.

Thank You, God, for gentle Ben,
for his quiet, forgiving, genuinely humble soul.
He never "put on airs;" he walked in his integrity.
His door was always open to dignitary and student,
ambassador and child,
all equally welcomed.
Lord, how he loved people... and liked them
respected them and **needed** them.
They... we... were food for his spirit,
holy communion, the sacrament of human love.
He remembered everybody's name; he never forgot a face.

You enriched our lives beyond measure
in Your gift of Ben to our world,
and we have a treasury of images:
Ben lugging a typewriter up flight after flight of stairs
for a student at Yale
or, our rushing to the hospital to visit the sick
and being greeted at the door by Ben,
who'd already been there and administered the
first rites of friendship
...memories of too much need and too few resources
and his somehow always finding the funds –
generously, quietly, often personally.
We see Ben presiding graciously at grand occasions,
commencements, convocations.
How he loved and appreciated rituals, ceremonies,
parties, festivals. Did anyone ever celebrate better?
We can see him now at his first festival here –
the Festival of Childhood – all dressed up as his favorite,
Winnie-the-Pooh,
in that magnificent, hot costume.
He was the most jovial Renaissance King and jolly round
Santa of all!

There he is at church, there at yet another soccer game, at every
recital, exhibition, meeting, memorial service,
caring so clearly about everything we did, large or small.

We pray, God of Presence –
be most near to Ben's beloved family:
to Betty,
dear, fragile, strong Betty…
to Andy and Grace and Mary and George… to their families…
the children… and all our extended family.
Help us to honor Ben
by savoring life
and doing good
and doing well,
by being of good cheer within and of real service without.
Help us to heed every hint of an angel here,
a saint there,
an old friend coming in our door.
We hurt, but we do not despair.
We listen for the sounds of joy,
for the singing of the saints.
And we shall add our voices
to their choir…
so –
help us –
God!
Amen.

*   *   *   *   *

Sam Scoville, *who taught English and later became dean, remembers Ben when he first came to Warren Wilson:*

"Reuben Holden, bless his heart. One of my heroes, closest to
sainthood as far as I'm concerned. Gentle. Patient. The summer
we arrived, we lived right behind him. The day _he_ moved in, we

watched him stumble through the vines and branches between our houses to introduce himself and welcome us here."

The following vivid memory is from alum and minister **Jon Bliss***:*

"I've just driven 900 miles from New England in my Toyota pickup, and parked – probably illegally – in front of Gladfelter, a day late for freshman orientation.

A well-dressed white haired man with papers under his arm approaches.

'Jonathan – the drive down from Vermont must have been tiring! They're just starting to serve dinner. Let's see what's on the menu...'

There are many ways to be welcomed, and at Warren Wilson I began to understand the radical power of generosity, a student at the feet of so many gracious teachers. Their curiosity and kindness opened my life.

But those first few steps on College soil set the bar, as the white-haired gentleman, his hand still on my elbow, leads me into the dining hall, says a word to the student taking tickets, steers me past the salad bar, past the curious faces, and right up to the hamburgers and fries.

'We'll have two,' says Dr. Holden."

Alumna and coastal ecologist **Christine Laporte Gardiner** *recalls:*

"My five years (1981-1986) under the nurturing leadership of Ben Holden holds many memories – visiting him in his office with its open door policy, being swept up in his infectious chuckle and twinkling eyes, sensing his profound humanity through which he really could connect with anyone, and enjoying his and Betty's abiding hospitality at their home (where I often house-sat). There is also a litany of 'hidden' impacts that he had on my life via his work on behalf WWC and our broader community. But in my heart, my favorite memory of Ben is one in which his invisible presence was felt at critical times.

Based on his and other *ex-Yalies'* encouragement, I applied to the Yale School of Forestry and Environmental Studies, something I would not have pursued without his and Betty's belief in me. I was accepted. Just when the challenges of being in graduate school and working to support myself were nearly overwhelming, I would find a note in my Sage Hall mailbox at Yale from Ben. He would have been passing through New Haven, and I was astonished he took the time to try and find me to say hello and see how I was faring. This occurred numerous times; sadly we always missed each other, but those sweet notes and the thoughtfulness behind them kept me inspired to rise to the Yale occasion and do well in my graduate work. I am so lucky, proud and humbled to have known him and treasure those notes alongside my WWC degree signed by Ben."

The following is from WWC assistant registrar and alumna **Marion Yeager:**

"What can I say about Ben Holden that hasn't already been said? He was a sincere and warm and welcoming man. He was an inspirational leader. He would routinely sit at the cafeteria table with any student, staff, faculty or volunteer and enjoy the table conversation.

But before I knew these things, I visited WWC as a prospective student. My parents and I were given a campus tour and then an interview with an admissions counselor. Toward the end of our conversation, the admissions counselor picked up the phone to ask if the president of the college was available. He was, so my parents and I were invited to Dr. Holden's office to meet and greet. (Let me stop here and say that the campus tour alone had me hooked!) My heavens... how many schools treat their ordinary prospective students to a one-on-one with the president?! We were made to feel oh-so-special. And that was one of Ben Holden's many gifts – making individuals feel truly special and valued.

After I had become a student, I remember that we had some international visitors at the campus. One visitor in particular spoke no English whatsoever. Ben received the group with the customary decorum, and later took the one visitor aside by his elbow, walking amiably between Gladfelter and wherever they were going. Ben was talking to the man as if he could understand every word. Ben knew the man would understand the feeling of the conversation, even if he could not understand the words. This gesture of kindness and welcome made a tremendous impression on me.

I know for a fact that Ben Holden is remembered fondly by the thousands of students who passed through WWC during his tenure. He set an extraordinary example of compassionate leadership, one we can all learn from, no matter what our profession."

Ben Holden

BERNHARD LAURSEN

Fred and Gordon Mahy buried "Fessor" in our college cemetery when he died in 1972. The community joined together in the chapel for a memorial service, which celebrated his good life. Unfortunately, his file is the other one missing from Fred's folder, so I will try to tell his story:

The Laursen Annex to the Administration Building was named for BERNHARD and KATHRINE LAURSEN. They both were born in Denmark. Bernhard lost his father at age 9; after that life was a struggle. He lived with his mother and four siblings, two of whom died in infancy. Of his two remaining brothers, one died in World War I, the other in World War II. Bernhard went to the University of Bonn to study agriculture, learn English, and get a degree. **Ernst and Pat Laursen** *tell me that by the time he came to America for a better life, he spoke five languages. He became a citizen as soon as he could, because he believed if you live here you should fully belong.*

Bernhard and Kathrine met in a small Danish Lutheran church in Boston. It was there they found out about the Farm School from George and Marguerite Butler Bidstrup, who ran the John C. Campbell Folk School in Brasstown, North Carolina. They thought Bernhard would be a perfect fit at the Farm School. So in 1931, after working in Boston (and Kathrine in New York), the newly married twosome came south. Doc and Thekla Jensen attended that same church, as did Doc's parents, and it was through this church and Bernhard that the Jensens heard of Warren Wilson.

Dr. Henry "Sherfey" Randolph, *Superintendent of the Farm*

School, had this to say of Bernhard: "Mr. Laursen is a man of rare abilities along many lines. His experiences in Europe have made him a great peace advocate. He believes we are in a tremendous job here in the mountains, a job just begun. He also believes that National Missions is just now in its prime and is needed more now than ever before. His strong body, skillful hands and trained mind, make him a master of any situation. Consequently, he is admired and followed by all who know him. His personality is charming. Those who see him or hear him always want more of him." Ernst and Pat recall that Dr. Randolph sent Bernhard on the road, traveling extensively for the college, visiting and speaking in churches as far west as California. His main mission was to raise awareness to support National Missions of the Presbyterian Church.

After serving in other capacities – running the paint crew, training teams in gymnastics and tumbling, coaching basketball, and leading folk dancing, then called "singing games" – Bernhard took over the position of farm manager. He was a country boy at heart. Years later he was succeeded by his son, Ernst. Bernhard loved the land and soon, under his careful supervision, the farm had grown into one of the most respected in North Carolina.

Kathrine was the dietitian, cook, and ran the cafeteria when it was located in the basement of Sunderland and then moved it to Gladfelter after it was built. Both Bernhard and Kathrine were known for their no-nonsense work ethic, their absolute honesty, and their great Danish pastry. Everyone always looked forward to the special times their pastry was served, and their crews were always among the hardest working on campus.

Bernhard was a strong, well built man with a bald, shiny head. He ran a tight "farm" ship, believed in hard, well-done work, but also loved to tease. He had a twinkle in his eye, a captivating smile, and a nickname for everyone. Students were honored and felt special when they received a moniker from him, and he seemed to know the ones who most needed it. Campus-wide he was known by his own nickname "Fessor," origin unknown (probably short for "professor").

Fessor is the person who began the Warren Wilson Thanksgiving tradition of bringing the farm display to the church service on the Sunday before Thanksgiving. He had an artist's eye, and each year thereafter he created something remarkably beautiful to delight the congregation. Using cornstalks, grains, pumpkins and gourds, and every natural growing thing to make it beautiful, the first display was located in Sunderland where the church service took place before the Elizabeth Williams Chapel was built.

This lovely display grew proportionately each year of Fessor's tenure. Many truly magnificent creations delighted congregations. Live animals were eventually added to the displays. Over the years I remember a small cow in the chancel, several geese, countless turkeys, a sow, and a plethora of piglets. I must be forgetting others, but I do remember some not using their "church voices"!

Son Ernst inherited his father's artistic eye and gift to create, and the displays continued to grow in the years following... until eventually they occupied the entire chancel and part of the narthex in the "new chapel on the hill" (the present-day chapel). Fred and I both thought that all we really needed to do on these special Sundays was just sit in the pew and let the beauty speak. Words were not needed, although we used them.

Fessor died fifteen years before Kathrine, who remained living near the campus – a beloved member of the community, keeping a watchful eye on her son, the farm manager – and still making her Danish pastry.

Fred called Bernhard and Kathrine's daughters-in-law, "daughters-in-love." Ernst's wife **Pat Laursen***, who was for many years WW's alumni director, said the following: "I think they were two of the most open and caring people I have ever known. Their love, caring and respect for the students and staff was unbounded. Whatever was asked of them – they stepped forward and did it. Their home was always open and always filled with visitors. Students and staff returned to visit them often."*

Bernhard Laursen

KATHRINE LAURSEN

THESE WERE THE WORDS SPOKEN AT HER SERVICE IN 1987:

Kathrine Wisborg was born on April 5, 1899 in Denmark, one of 16 children. She was apprenticed as a dietician and emigrated in 1920, leaving the beauty and comfort of Denmark for the adventure and opportunism of America. She lived and worked in Boston and New York, where she met a young man named Bernhard Laursen in the youth group of the Danish Lutheran church. She attended Dana College, learned English, married "Fessor," and they came to Swannanoa intending to stay "just a while." In Kathrine's case just a little while turned into 56 years. She worked as a dietician at the Farm School, Asheville Teacher's College, Warren Wilson, and after retirement, Swannanoa School and Owen High. She and Bernhard were with Warren Wilson for 40 years. Kathrine is survived and loved by her two sons, five grandchildren, one great-granddaughter and many friends.

We are here to worship God, to remember and honor Kathrine Laursen, her death, her life, her influence on our lives.

AS FRED PRAYED FOR KATHRINE:

O God, before whom generations rise and pass away,
we praise You for all Your servants who, having lived life faithfully,
with grace,
live eternally with You,
and those they loved who went before,

and in our memories.
We praise You for giving us Kathrine Laursen.
We are grateful that her life was as good as it was long,
and that her dying was not too hard.
We can't imagine the shifts she lived through from the last century
in Denmark,
to now – here,
the profound changes she experienced, took in,
became in her 88 years of living.
Each of us remembers her from our own experience with her,
a long time ago or just last week – as mother, mother-in-law, sister, grandmother, colleague, friend.
We saw her in as many ways as we are persons.
She was all of that and so much more – daughter, child, young
girl, old woman,
public, private, as we knew her, as she is fully known to You.

We remember her with great gratitude and fond, fond love –
her honesty, candor, blunt impatience with hypocrisy or games.
You could always count on her to say what she meant, to mean
what she said
and to be open and real and authentic.
She was, Lord, herself, like no other, such a force, such a person.

She fed us all with great Danish pastry, delicious bread and rolls,
and vast amounts of love.
She turned Sunderland basement into her dining room, and it became, with little modern equipment and great old-fashioned giving,
a joy to enter, a place to learn,
where generations of students were nourished.
We remember her generosity, her courage, her pride in her heritage, in her work,
in her children – so many children, who came back year after year
to see her.
Her orphaned sons will miss her more than they can yet possibly
know.

Her daughters in — love have lost a mother.
Her grandchildren have lost Bestamore (Best-amor)
as have we all.
But we do not grieve — because she was who she was, because You
are God and Jesus didn't lie, because if we can possibly believe in
this incredible, beautiful, heart-rending, grace-full LIFE, that we
should live at all,
then that we should live forever should really not surprise us.
O God, You have blessed us on our way from our mother's arms
in this world, into the next
then . . . . now . . . . . evermore
Thank You, God, for everything.
Amen.

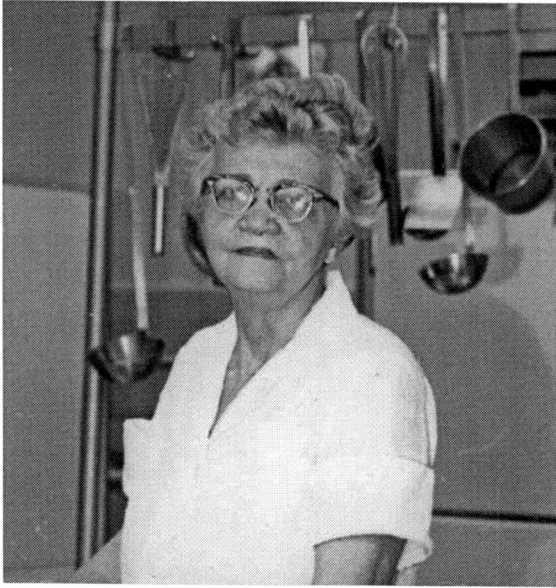

Kathrine Laursen

SAMUEL DeVRIES

Devries Gym is named for SAM DeVRIES. When we came to campus, he was heading the work program and was in charge of maintaining the buildings and grounds of the campus as well as the vehicles of the college. He was the person first out in a snowstorm plowing the roads or scraping the chapel and classroom building steps to keep us safe. He was a hard worker with a strong mid-western ethic, honorable to his core. In earlier years he had coached several different Farm School and Warren Wilson sport teams, so everyone still called him, "Coach."

Coach was a large, handsome man from Nebraska. There were many coaches in the history of the college, but this man was THE coach who kept that name until long after he retired, up until he died. His wife, Evelyn, was the postmistress, and as I write this she is about to celebrate her 100th birthday in the summer of 2010.

Everyone loved and respected them both. If anyone had a problem in a campus house or classroom, the repeated advice was to "Call Coach!" I think he was on constant call.

Coach was demanding of his workers, but was also deeply respected by them. They worked hard to please him and took good care of the college property. Even the most belligerent students said when he was angered, his bark was worse than his bite.

I've seen his eyes sparkle happily after eating his daily ice cream treat, or in his lovely home entertaining graciously with his adored wife, who also was a remarkable cook and most delightful hostess. Evelyn had an amusing sense of humor that made us laugh and always lit up Sam's handsome face.

Another faithful churchman and elder, Coach dedicated his life to the college. He worked tirelessly for Warren Wilson his whole working career, serving on many important college and church committees. He was always attentive to all our teams and encouraged the new coaches and athletes. Coach was 80 when he died.

AT THE 1991 SERVICE FOR SAM DeVRIES, THESE WERE FRED'S OPENING WORDS:

"There were giants in the earth in those days," says the Bible
in describing the sacred past.
There were giants in the earth in our days as well.
One of the patriarchs of Warren Wilson,
one of the pillars of our temple, master builder, gentle giant,
Sam DeVries is dead.
That's why we're here – to face his death and to remember his life.
For 57 years he lived here, worked here, loved here,
and left his mark all around us and deep within us.
Let us thank God, honor Sam, support each other, pray and sing,
and worship God.

INVOCATION:

Three score and ten. Lord, by reason of strength – four score.
We are grateful for Sam – grateful that his cancer is overcome,
all restraints are removed; his work is complete, his dying done,
and he is born again to resurrection, to life eternal –
near to Your heart, precious to our hearts.
He has lost the earth he knew for greater knowing,
his life for greater life, left the friends he loved for greater loving –
"to find a land larger than earth."
We who remain on earth, living this life, amid these friends,
knowing in part –
resolve to extend our awareness, to deepen our gratitude,

to widen our love – that, in faith
we shall more and more know as we are known,
and live, as we are loved – through Christ our Lord.
Amen.

WORDS OF REMEMBRANCE:

I cannot think of Sam without thinking of work. He was, among
so many other things, the director of the work program at the college. All his life he worked hard and well and long. He embodied
the Calvinist work ethic.

He also did what he loved and loved what he did. In Robert Frost's
words, he "united his avocation with vocation,"
"love and need" were one, his labor was done "for heaven's and the
future's sake."

Sam's faith was en-acted, done, worked out,
Incarnated.

Noel McInnis has written:
    "There are two ways to find your livelihood.
    One is to look at all the slots that others have assigned
    and choose one, endure the maze of preparations
    that others have set up for you to get you there. This is the way
    for those
    who are content to have their livelihood sustain whatever life
    remains.
    The other is to look into yourself and nurture what you find
    most worthy there,
    and grow into some of the unfulfilled space that others have not
    frozen.
    There is always more room for one more space,
    and since all spaces are the trace of some event
    why not a space invented by yourself?
    This is the way of those never content 'til livelihood and life are

both the same."

PRAYER FOR COACH:

Lord, we remember and we celebrate a man, a man's man,
a woman's man, a one-woman man —
strong, modest, steady.
A missionary from a family of missionaries
sent from the plains of Nebraska to this good valley.
Coach, the original Coach,
who loved and taught so many of us to coach others,
elder, taskmaster — (we can almost hear the rumble in his voice
when faced with sloppiness or laziness,
confronting a student or a colleague leaving his tools lying
around,
not cleaning up his brushes, leaving the teaching unfinished).
We recall his impatience with excuses —
AND his gracious forgiveness, the courage of his convictions,
so solid — so Dutch,
the depth of his love.
He helped so many people, with his resources, with his hands,
with his encouragement, with his support —
out of sight, quietly, modestly.
He had so many children, and to this day his surrogate sons rise
up
to call him blessed —
boys whom he coached, mentored, befriended, helped,
who have become good men because of Sam.
This whole crazy, blessed place bears his mark wherever we turn —
in the shops, on the roads, the gym, the walls,
the very stones in this chapel carry his fingerprints,
witness his labor, speak his life.

We pray for Evelyn, his wife, his friend, his love.
Be, O God, real to her when she is courageous and when she weeps
alone — at a loss for words or presence or faith.

Be, O Lord, real to her when she is strong and when she is not.
Remind her that her pain is eloquent profound testimony to their
love.
May Your love welcome her grief, honor its honesty
and raise it to a joy she cannot yet imagine or believe possible.
We, her sisters and family and friends shall add our love to Yours
– for her.
We pray for Sam's sisters, his brother, all his family, his friends,
for ourselves.
May our work be half as true as his,
our faith just as strong,
our lives – so full.
In the name of the Lord of life.
Amen.

Coach DeVries

ANNETTE SCHAFER

Schafer Dormitory burned to the ground, but lo and behold it was built again in the same place, looking a little different but still called Schafer – named for ANNETTE SCHAFER, secretary to Dr. Bannerman, who first came to Warren Wilson in 1936. We knew her well and shared common New York beginnings.

In that first internship year at Warren Wilson she was our closest neighbor and dear friend. We lived in an already-condemned house located on the slant between Sunderland and the infirmary, right under the siren that loudly announced every meal time and the beginning and ending of work. In that crazy little house, we teased each other throughout that year, and her delightful sense of humor evoked so much laughter and great fun. She was a dedicated churchwoman who lived her faith daily and with genuine joy. Her entire working life was devoted to the college.

We loved welcoming her to New Haven to see the Yale campus the year after our internship. She wanted to see where we lived and I think make sure we were all right, so she visited us on her vacation, spent a few nights in out guest room and I'm sure reported back to our friends on the WW campus that we were doing just fine without them (although we missed them all dearly because they already felt like part of our family). What a devoted friend Annette was.

IN FRED'S WORDS AT HER SERVICE IN 1984:

When Beverly and I first arrived here in 1955 for my internship from Yale Divinity School, the second person we met after Dr. Bannerman was Annette Schafer, Art's secretary. Together with

Jenny Lewis, she was our downstairs neighbor in Teacher's Cottage. Annette greeted us warmly, graciously, and made us feel instantly at home in that old ramshackle building long since gone. We shared the termites, the sagging timbers, Annette's floor dropping one day a foot or more away from the walls from wood rot, the toadstools growing out of her bathroom floor.

She put up with a lot from me – like the time I caught a sunfish and sneaked it into her bathtub, or the time the good women of the church were meeting downstairs in her apartment for Wednesday night prayer meeting and had gotten very quiet for circle prayers, and their praying was just about destroyed by loud thumping sounds from our apartment above, raucous ungodly sounds as a student and I were listening to Dave Brubeck and thumping our feet to the rhythm. I know it happened, not because Annette complained, but because this preacher's red-faced, young wife was trying to pray below.

All of us could share an hour's worth of memories about Annette's driving adventures. The Keener children used to cry out, "Watch out, here comes Miss Schafer in the blue bomb!" I can still see her attempting a turn off Route 70 to the college road with left blinker on in the right lane, with a smile on her face and cars going in every direction, stopping, being thoroughly confused. My favorite memory is of the snowy night Annette drove the Comet up to Sage Circle for a meeting, when the trees in the circle were still saplings, and came in a little flustered, wondering to Evelyn Jones whether she may have strayed from the road a bit. When they went outside to look it was just like the cartoon you see in the *New Yorker* (usually linked with skiing) where you see a tree and tracks in the snow one on each side of it. Here was the snowy Sage Circle, with two tracks on either side of the tree, and Annette had driven over the sapling. It snapped back and stands to this day.

Annette's driving – and more seriously, her whole life – were sure and convincing evidence to me of the presence and reality of guardian angels, for Annette certainly had one.

Annette Schafer was old-fashioned. That is, a lady — proper and gracious, kind and gentle, discrete and dedicated, caring and faithful, a missionary from Brooklyn to Appalachia, who dedicated her life to her faith and her work to her Lord. She signed our checks, kept our minutes — and our secrets — worked long hours without complaint, gave generously of her skimpy salary and great heart to Dorland Bell, the Farm School, Warren Wilson College and the church. When she had to retire at 73, she said, "I really would be happier if I could go to the office every day." And even after she couldn't work and her mind shifted to a different dimension, she kept faithfully sewing clothes for children overseas. And always, she prayed for us, and cared about us, and loved us dearly.

Annette used to bother me in the early years of my severe Calvinism. I would preach sermons or lecture in class on sin, total depravity, the great pride that lurked in the depths of all of us, the terrible secret darkness in even the saints, and then I'd go home and see Annette, a living exception to my dark doctrines. How, thank God, she confounded me! Not that she was sinless, she of all people knew better. But, if ever there was a good person, a faithful conscientious servant of the Lord, it was Annette Schafer.

And even when she "sinned" and played cards, it was her favorite game —

Pennies from Heaven.

A PRAYER AT THE END OF THE SERVICE:

Lord, we really cannot grieve — because she hasn't been herself for a while now, and we're glad she's gone home to You to see clearly. We really cannot grieve because death was a release for her and for her friends and for her special friend, who went faithfully every week to sit with her long after (at least on the surface) Annette didn't know her anymore. We really cannot grieve because she was Annette, as good as they come — greeted we are sure with "Well done, good and faithful servant." We really cannot grieve because she loved the Lord, and You are her God more loving than ever she could imagine. We thank You and praise You for Your gift of her to us. Her faithful work, life-time service, her trusting, sweet soul and each of us here, and those who could not be here, and those who have gone on ahead, treasure special memories, unfeigned appreciation and a great debt to dear, dear Annette.

Annette Schafer

JOHN CONNET

JOHN CONNET was the director of music when we arrived at Warren Wilson. He led the choir in all the church services; he WAS the music department in the college, teaching all the courses. He directed quite a professional performance of H.M.S. PINAFORE using our student talent on stage and in the orchestra. He and his wife, Mickey, his daughter, Joan, and two sons, Bill and Pete, lived on the first floor of Randolph House and were our neighbors. They had found their place just right and were valued members of the community – when tragedy struck on one ordinary, sunny morning in the spring of 1962.

A vehicle, temporarily parked higher on the road, rolled backward down the hill as John was crossing the road reading his mail, returning from the post office to his office in Spidel. It hit him, killing him instantly. There were many witnesses to the disaster and help was immediate, but John had died and there was no way to bring him back. The community was deeply affected by John's death and mourned with profound grief along with the Connet family. **Betty Nelson,** *who as a student was witness to the accident, remembers a most poignant scene shortly after. John's son, Pete, was responsible for raising and lowering the flag each day on the flagpole near the formal garden. She said she would never forget the sight of watching young Pete lowering the flag to half-mast for his father. When she thinks about it, it still brings tears to her eyes.*

It's sad to me that John's death is so prevalent in our memories that we tend to forget what a dedicated teacher and musician he was. His choirs were wonderfully taught and directed, his dedication to the college was unsurpassed. He and Mickey gave their talents, their energy and their devotion to Warren Wilson and all that it was about. They were a family who would have remained as many years as the others, almost doubling their 24 years if the fates had allowed – doing their part, continuing to help the college grow and become.

The pipe organ in the Warren Wilson Presbyterian Church and College Chapel is named in memory of John Connet.

Mickey lived a long life and remained an active member of the Warren Wilson Church and College Chapel. The children went on to college, married, had children, and Joan, after graduating from Duke, worked for our college for a short time.

THESE WERE FRED'S WORDS IN THE ELIZABETH WILLIAMS CHAPEL SHORTLY AFTER JOHN'S DEATH in 1962:

We are all reminded, at such a time as this
of something we all tend to forget – and remove –
and do not want to know –
the reality
the certainty
the shadow of death.
Suddenly the "important" trivialities vanish,
the insignificant disappears,
and we stand face to face with ultimate reality,
the deepest concern,
the real issue of life and death.
And we know how fleeting and mysterious and precious
and tenuous
life on this strange, beautiful earth really is.
What we feel most immediately is confusion,
loss, sorrow.
Do not be ashamed of those feelings,
for we are human and mortal, and such it is to be a person.
Jesus too walked this valley,
and therefore God understands.

But, we are here to move beyond mourning
because we remember who John Connet was.
I shall not recall to You the events of his life,
nor try to measure the statue of the man.
In the first place, because, any life is so very much more
than fact and word and record,
and also, because we who are gathered here are not strangers, but
friends –
his friends
and his death was a death in the family.
But, I would remind You of one thing – the quality of his life.
John, on many occasions would share with me his convictions.
If one thing seemed crucially important to him, it was stewardship.
He saw all of life as a gift to be given back in joy and service.
He understood the worship of music.
He poured out his talents and time and self here for twenty-four
years.
And outside this community
enriching worship and the lives of countless folk.
We remember not a wasted life, but a full one, an expression of
what he dearly believed.
John Connet was a good steward –
as a son
husband,
father,
teacher,
musician,
friend,
man,
Christian.
We feel more than sorrow and loss
for we remember the quality of his life, and who he was.
But even more because
we remember who God is:
abiding, eternal,

but, that is not enough.
Death is so strong – it separates and removes.
There is one thing greater – stronger...
Love.
Death has been overcome by love.

Will we know loss? Of course.
Shall we weep? Yes.
But, rejoice,
worship,
Easter is today!

*　*　*　*　*

Alumna **Maryam Daftari** *is an accomplished musician; these are her fond memories of her music teacher and friend:*

"John Connet was a great favorite of mine when I came to Warren Wilson in 1961 from Tehran, Iran. He loved music, and that was a large part of his life. Music was my love also, so we hit it off from the very beginning. He was always kind, full of energy, very enthusiastic in all he did and said, very positive and caring, always ready to lend a helping hand. I helped him in choir by playing the piano for choir practices. I remember those precious times fondly. He was a great music teacher, devoted to his art and to his students. He put his whole being into his conducting and his music. And every student felt his bubbling energy and fervor.

He did me a great service, which affected my entire musical life. He introduced me to Mrs. Grace Potter Carroll, a great pianist in Asheville who installed the Helen Wu Piano Scholarship for one music student every two years. Whoever won the scholarship had free lessons with Mrs. Carroll every week for two years. Several students competed (taken by John Connet to Mrs. Carroll), and I was the lucky one chosen by her.

These lessons were some of the most precious moments in my entire life, for I learned from a master teacher and musician. She had a special love for the heavenly piano music of Robert Schumann and she conveyed this love to me. And all this was because of the kindness and thoughtfulness of John Connet, who encouraged me to go and sit for the competition and gave me the courage to think that I could win.

The deep pain of his untimely and tragic death, I can never forget. I mourned for months. I missed him, for he was not only a great music teacher, but a very dear friend. I was away from home, but I knew I could talk to him, confide in him, and pour my heart out. He had always been there for me, to listen like a friend, like a father. His memory remains dear to me."

John Connet

DWIGHT VINING

In the decade after World War II, Army Surplus provided very inexpensive materials to non profit institutions. DWIGHT VINING's non-profit card was used often when supplies were needed. We wondered once why all the classrooms were painted the same not-too-pleasant shade of green. When it was explained that Mr. Vining got a very good price on the paint if he bought a very large supply, we knew that we'd better get used to the color!

He was thrifty for the good of the college. We never operated in the red when he was in charge. Having gone through the Depression, he learned well how to spend wisely, and often if some household project needed refurbishing, his wife, Allie B., was there with needle and thread or wallpaper paste, freely giving of her time and talent to assist her fugal husband. He was a very ethical mid-westerner with a penchant for doing things right.

I loved knowing that it was his idea to work out a deal with a movie theater manager in Asheville to "borrow" a film on Saturday nights to show to the campus students who had no way off campus. He knew they were in need of entertainment. Of course, there was o television, so Mr. Vining drove to Asheville to pick up the film and then again to return it. He never got much praise for doing that, so I'm thanking him now. He was a very nice man.

1N 1999 WHEN DWIGHT VINING DIED, FRED WROTE THIS ABOUT HIM:

Vining. Vining Dormitory. Students say the name every day, but few here remember the man in whose honor the dorm was named. Dwight Vining was one of those "stalwart pioneers" who helped to shape Warren Wilson College, a vital forefather of our heritage.

Dwight Vining was Warren Wilson's business manager; he was elected and re-elected clerk of session for this church; he served for many years as the stated clerk of Holston Presbytery. As the college's chief financial officer, he ran a tight and leak-free ship. He made you defend the expenditure of every penny but we were never in debt, except to his good stewardship. His desk was a mess, a stunning disorder in the midst of Dwight's decent and orderly life. But ask him for an invoice, and he would go down into the pile and find it in a moment.

Every week, he would obtain a 35 mm film from an Asheville movie theater to show the free Saturday night flick on campus. Whether he approved of the film or not, he would run the projector from the booth at the back of the old Williams Chapel and look with amazement at the audience below – a motley crew of students from the Farm School (later Warren Wilson High School and Junior College) and Black Mountain College, that nearby experimental/radical hotbed whose students looked and lived, fifty years ago, like our students do today.

As the church's clerk of session, Dwight kept fair and meticulous minutes, and his knowledge of church law and practice of Christian ethics were incomparable. As the stated clerk of Presbytery, he was our historian and parliamentarian, the rudder that kept that blessed ship of fools afloat. Preachers and moderators came and went; he stayed and served.

Dwight was from Kansas. With his handsome, fine white hair, he stood as erect and dignified as an elder in a Grant Wood painting. He and his wife, Allie B., were very different from each other, true complements, and very devoted. Dwight was a loving husband and a deeply caring father and grandfather. He was a conservative in the very best sense of that word, a gentle man of integrity

96

and conscience. He was liberal in his patience with those far to his left religiously or politically, treating all people with conviction, courtesy, decency and respect. Dwight Vining was a very good person who lived a life as true as it was long. He was one of our patriarchs, and we thank God for the gift of this noble man.

Dwight Vining

Dwight Vining

LEON DESCHAMPS

The DESCHAMPS were just ending their working years when we first became part of WWC, but they lived nearby and Fred always enjoyed their visits and conversations. When we came back to the campus to stay in 1958, we lived in a house that Mr. Deschamps had designed and built. Preston was a lovely house to live in with a round stone fireplace and solid cement walls. Our children were babies in that house, which give it special memories.

We always respected and admired the many talents of the Deschamps, and I still have and treasure the intricately made cornhusk dolls that May Deschamps made. Her work was good enough to be in the Smithsonian... and it is! She belonged to the famous singing Ritchie family of Kentucky, who sang at her service. The Deschamps were lovely, gentle people who worked hard and gave freely of their talents.

FROM THE 1986 SERVICE ABOUT HIS LIFE:

A PRAYER FOR LEON:

Leon Deschamps was as fine a gentleman as You ever created —
Oh, God and we thank You and remember
his honesty, his humor,
his impatience with nonsense, especially ecclesiastical nonsense,
his deep and daily prayer life, his wisdom and his integrity,
his delight in a good discussion,
his concern for those around him, even when he was in pain.

They Faithfully Led the Way

He was so distinctly European, so charmingly Belgian and American –
that "fine man from off," who came to Kentucky
with a twinkle in his smile and found love.
Artist, engineer, forester, builder, colonel, teacher,
principal, man of principles,
we celebrate his 94 good and giving years.

I and everyone who ever lived in his solid, true and
welcoming houses, thank You for his gifts.
Those who became and grew up and grew out from the home that
he and May loved into being – his children, his grandchildren,
his great grandchildren, bless You for him.

We also thank You for death.
Our earthly bodies were not made to last forever –
they grow tired and worn and ready –
and we are grateful that when our work is done,
Christ takes us home to glad re-union,
we give back to nature only that which is natural,
to the grave only that which the grave can hold.
To You we give our very souls – and his.
Amen.

Leon Deschamps

MAY RITCHIE DESCHAMPS

FROM THE 1982 SERVICE ABOUT HER LIFE:

A PRAYER FOR MAY:

Lord, it is not easy — not even when a life was as long and rich, as
gracious, strong and gentle as May's.
It may even be harder to believe she's left us on this side of glory,
for she seemed so — forever.
So, Father, receive our very human, totally honest grief
now and in the days to come.

Receive also our thanksgiving,
we thank You for life and for all that makes life so good, so very
good.
We thank You that You set us in families
and draw us out of our loneliness
by ties of kin and ties of friendship.
We thank You for father love and mother love,
for the love of husband and wife and sister and brother
and children and grandchildren, great grandchildren.
We thank You, from our hearts, for May —
daughter sister, wife,
"who met that fine man from off"
Lord, she once said, a long time ago,
"I guess it was a good thing I made a start for the others."
We know so.
Her husband, her children, her family and friends
rise up and call her blessed, and a blessing —

in Clear Creek, Viper, Pine Mountain, Brasstown, Swannanoa.
We see again her hands, which worked so hard,
with such care and craft and artistry,
taking the simple and making it stunning,
sending her little people and great love around the world.
We hear her voice in song and serenity,
we see that face, that beautiful face,
and we rejoice for her long, faithful, gentle, loving life
grateful for her faith in the Lord,
and grateful that her suffering is over and that she knows what we
but glimpse.
We are grateful that her work on earth is done and You have taken
her home.
In Jesus name, for no better name do we know.
Amen.

As a prelude to the Ritchie family singing at the service, Fred quoted Jean, May's sister, who said –

"Best of all the singing."

"No matter how far apart we might scatter the world over, we'll still be the Ritchie family as long as we lived and sang the same old songs and that the songs would live as long as there was a family."

May Deschamps

ELIZABETH MARTIN

Not many people knew her name was ELIZABETH, because to most she was known as "Bidge." Of course, students in the early years were much more proper and always referred to her as MISS MARTIN. I'm not sure exactly when that change happened, when we were suddenly all called by our first names, as is the norm today.

What a wonderful combination she was of hard worker – totally efficient in every role she undertook – and comedian. She was so dignified AND so funny. It took a while to discover her funny side, but it was definitely there. She loved to make us laugh and we respected her all the more for it.

Bidge had so many personas as you discover as you read further. She was such a distinctive, respected, trusted friend to so many students and staff – a wise administrator, teacher, woman.

FROM HER MEMORIAL SERVICE IN 1990:

BIOGRAPHICAL SKETCH:

Elizabeth was born on October 31, 1903 in Pittsburgh, Pennsylvania. From the beginning of her life, she had ties to Presbyterian colleges. Her father was president of Wilson College in Pennsylvania, her mother, dean of students. Elizabeth graduated from Wilson College and Columbia University and taught in private schools in New England, Wisconsin and New Jersey before coming to Warren Wilson College in 1949. During her long service, she taught math full-time, was assistant dean, dean of women, and registrar of the college.

A fine athlete herself, she coached woman's basketball when the coach left and it was the only sport available to women. In her "spare time," she slept a little. As the college statistician, she helped Dr. Jensen write the first history of the college, she wrote the first history of the Warren Wilson Church, of which she was a member for 40 years, an elder, president of the women's association, active in synod, presbytery and editor of the church's *Extended Family* newsletter.

In her honor, awards have been established to the work program of the college.

Bidge died unexpectedly, quietly and mercifully. We are here today to worship God and to honor her, our respected colleague, our loved friend.

REMEMBRANCE:

Elizabeth Martin was a mathematician, a meticulous keeper of records, grades, history, facts. There was that side of her (dean, registrar, elder, Calvinist) that was demanding, rigorous, no-nonsense. She was no easy sell, no soft touch. And how she cared — for Warren Wilson College, for people, for students — especially the troubled, the inept, the vulnerable. Barbara Hempleman once said that one of her earliest images of Miss Martin, when she first came to Warren Wilson to teach math and — in Dr. Bannerman's words, "help with student government" — is a picture of her in Stephenson, listening to a student. Her head inclined toward the speaker, stance relaxed and accepting, brow furrowed with concentration. She really listened — and listened for years — to students, staff, friends, visitors. Then she'd ask a question, one that went right to the point, or to the weakness in an argument. The brow might be furrowed, but the eyes twinkled. Oh, how they twinkled.

Elizabeth Martin was also 'Bidge,' and Bidge was one of the funniest persons I have ever known. She had a wit and grace that was
the sense of humor. Who of us who were ever there could forget her
presentation of the scholar's medals on Honors and Awards Night
near the end of a long and serious string of presentations when Bidge
– the Mother Goose of Honors and Awards would preface the medals with her poetry – fey and funny and marvelous?

She often surprised me by the acceptance and tolerance and
sheer grace that she showed me and other students. To this day,
I am convinced that by the grace of God and the mercy of Bidge,
a student who had made a career of flunking basic math finally
passed it and graduated.

She loved to see the other side, to travel the road less worn, to
buck trends and resist the obvious. She loved the overlooked, the
passed-by, the wearing out ones. I shall never forget the poem she
wrote on the day we dedicated this chapel and I wrote an "Ode"
to this new, beautiful church. She wrote "Old Chapel," and it was
about the old Elizabeth Williams Building and aging and remembrance, and tradition and gratitude decency:

"I passed the chapel standing in the rain
at least it *was* the chapel until today.
It looked so tired and a bit forlorn,
like some old man who'd had his day.
I thought back to the many, many,
the college generations now for thirty years
who'd felt drawn to that place,
sometimes by edict of requirement,
sometimes to see a talent show,
or a movie date on Saturday,
but often by a deep desire to worship God
each in his own way, his inmost heart...

They Faithfully Led the Way

Did the old chapel feel a twinge of jealousy
of that new beauteous structure on the hill?
Did its worn seats and termite ridden beams
feel older, squeakier, shabbier today?
It seems to me it did look tired and worn,
but thankful too that new life was there
to carry the burden it had borne
through many a torrid summer day
rain pelting on the roof to silence even the most ardent preacher,
through many chilly winter night,
radiators pounding a loud crescendo.
Yes it had done its part, and the new church
was its direct descendant, its own son?
So, it was glad, though tinged with sadness too,
to have the worship carried on by stronger hands."

E.G. Martin   May 3rd 1964

Bidge Martin was a mother of this college, one of its true foundations.
She was a good and faithful member of this church through all
these years.
Our debt to her is immeasurable,
Our respect and our love are palpable.
She was a unique person, a great soul, one of a kind.
I shall miss her very much.

PRAYER:

When she was born, Lord, she wasn't expected to live.
She DID, thank You – how she did!
Fourscore and six and more and more.
We wish we'd be better prepared at the end – she wasn't to die.
We wish we could have said goodbye, but that's selfish.
We are glad that she was spared another bout –

a long painful bout with cancer. She fought that foe before and won.
Our joy transcends our sorrow because she lived long
and with such dignity, such integrity, such serious fun.
Our joy transcends our sorrow because she was a liberated woman,
a free human being for as long as we knew her, a Christian.
Comfort her nieces and nephews, her closest friends, all her friends,
and hear our praise for her vision,
for all she did and how she lived
and who she was.

Bidge Martin

WILLIAM KLEIN

Of all those who found their way to Warren Wilson College, BILL and BETTY KLEIN were possibly the most perfect match to all its ambiance — beyond image, to the core of the best it was trying to be. They believed in community, equality, and caring, and were themselves the epitome of goodness. Bill had more degrees than anyone on campus — five, I think, from the very best schools, and his title Dr. could have been Rev. Dr. — but Bill hated titles and wanted to be just plain Bill.

He preferred his classes to be small and intimate. He did not like speaking to large groups, but never minded the camaraderie of the soccer team for which he was the assistant coach to Sam Millar for many years. He truly believed that playing with ethical sportsmanship was much more important than winning, but we won anyway and became national champions.

An anthropologist, Bill was the person who discovered the archeological dig on the campus and with his students worked it each summer, putting us on the map in that field with the connection to UNC Chapel Hill. For years, Ernst Laursen had been churning up bits of pottery when he plowed the fields to plant. When Bill discovered that, the archeological dig near the river on the bottom farmland began, and soon amazing finds were being discovered, Native American villages unearthed. I have a clear memory of the excitement when something new and important was excavated, when word traveled up to campus and many of us hastened down to the site to witness firsthand the artifact or the grave. The dig lasted many summers, and students in anthropology had a remarkable first-hand laboratory. Many of those artifacts were displayed in our own museum, which was housed in the old Williams Building (no longer standing), but the more valuable ones were sent to Chapel Hill where they are still kept.

Bill cared deeply for all of humanity and was often found comforting a student or dispelling a heated argument. He was a gentle peacemaker and healer.

Bill and Betty were genuine liberals who cared deeply and truly, who loved these mountains, the Appalachian culture and our college community in the midst of it. A perfectly matched couple, so loving and compatible, I can see them now – swinging around the gym floor, folk dancing in Bryson, doing all the proper steps, smiling and having so much fun. They were the first ones to introduce us to the Appalachia that they knew and respected and loved so well. When they took us to our very first Craftsman's Fair, they were so eager for us to meet those remarkable artisans from the mountains who handcrafted such extraordinary work. We were so very young and they were careful teachers. They imparted their love for this region to us city dwellers, two northern newcomers for whom everything here was an awakening.

After Betty died, Bill would often walk down the road to our house to bring a book or have a cup of tea and chat awhile. I loved his visits because I loved this man.

AT THE BEGINNING OF BILL'S MEMORIAL SERVICE IN 1975, FRED CALLED THE CONGREGATION TOGETHER BY SAYING:

We are here today because Bill Klein died. We bring our sorrow because we loved him, because he was a very good man, because we can't really quite believe it. We come that our distress may be sanctified, our gratitude expressed, our faith strengthened. We come to remember Bill and to worship God.

Then later in the service he prayed the following words:

Thank You, God, for Bill – son, husband, father, grandfather,

friend.
Thank You for the gift of his life to us and to so many others.
How can we measure it?

We remember with gratitude his talents –
scholar, teacher, theologian, scientist, coach, dancer, gentleman,
gentle – man.

We celebrate his humanism,
his lifelong search
("Here's a book you might enjoy." " Have you seen this article?"),
his anguish over grading one single student,
his understanding of,
love for,
incarnation of community.
None here ever cared more deeply,
or contributed more fully to Gemeinschaft.

We recall with joy – his strength, his limitless caring,
his love –
oh, how he did love,
his beautiful rapport with children
...and his humility.
Sometimes it annoyed us; often it judged our pride,
always it was real, compelling and profound.
He was a far better man than most of us – yet least aware of it.

And we celebrate his faith.
It was not an easy one,
for Bill was too wise and honest to believe blindly or without great
struggle.
But believe he did – deeply, compassionately, in the Lord
whom he studied and served and loved.
Therefore, our sorrow is turned into joy,
our mourning into dancing.

We shall not forget; we will build on his foundation.

* * * * *

Larry Adamson, *who taught biology at WWC and later became dean of students in the 1960's, remembers Bill this way:*

"In the fall of 1960 when we came to WWC, the Kleins, Adamsons and Ohlers sponsored the freshman class. This responsibility allowed us to form a friendship, which grew over time.

Bill built his department into one of the major academic offerings at WWC. He organized folk dancing, which was a major, positive activity for many of our students. I remember when we took students to gather rocks to be used in the building of the WW Church/Chapel. Bill was in there with the rest of us, carrying heavy rocks, even though he was getting older at that point. He always did his part and more.

When we were moving back to Texas and I was trying to get my office things to the house, Bill heard I was having a heard time securing a vehicle, brought his station wagon and helped me carry my things. Bill was so sensitive to others. He was one of the most giving, empathetic individuals I have ever known. He had a strong faith, which he lived in his gentle, unassuming way, but he was a tower of strength when defending injustice or someone who was not treated properly. Everyone loved him so much.

When I mentioned the giants of the campus, Bill should be included. He was one of God's best gifts to WWC – a beautiful man."

Alumna and teacher **Jewell Cardwell Field** *shares this about him:*

"I decided to become a sociology major because of the great

classes with Dr. Klein… I remember that he always wore a suit and tie, even on the soccer field, and looked like the perfect gentleman he was. He often had his students over to his house for hot chocolate in the winter, for root beer floats in the summer.

Woody Finley once shared with us a story of Dr. Klein's lecture to his soccer team after a particularly bad performance against the visiting opponent. He gathered the team around him and asked Woody to hold out a soccer ball. He pointed to it and said very seriously, 'Boys, this is a ball.' Dear man that he was, Dr. Klein found it very difficult to reprimand. There is actually a picture of this event in the 1956 OLE LADY (yearbook)."

Alumnus, minister, financier **Milton Ohlsen** *has this to say about what Dr. Klein taught him:*

"Bill Klein ruined my world! In response to a question in class, I replied, using as my foundation an article I had read in the newspaper. After all, newspapers don't lie. They are to be trusted to convey accurately the news of the day. As a young man who had been taught to always tell the truth, I certainly expected newspapers to be truthful as well.

In the space of that hour, Dr. Klein gently dashed my naiveté. After that, I never read much of anything trusting that it was the truth, the whole truth, and nothing but the truth. That gentle man opened my eyes, mind and heart without demeaning my mental capacity or me. Rather, he led me to a door and slowly opened it to allow me to see the world as it was and invited me to be able to critique and comprehend on a much higher level rather than simply, gullibly, ingesting 'stuff.'

The ability to think critically and to seek the 'truth,' for me, started during one class, with a gentle man leading me towards a door that some never see."

Bill Klein

ELIZABETH KLEIN

WHEN BETTY DIED IN 1970, FRED HONORED HER THIS WAY:

Grateful – for the beauty of the earth, for spring, for flowers, for life all around and going on as though nothing has happened? Oh God, it is hard at times, impossible, and we have wanted to cry out in resentment and hurt – stay the laughter and the sunshine & life as usual for death has come again and as though for the first time.

Death never, ever easy and we are ever, always vulnerable and we loved her and we miss her, her death matters, hurts, leaves a great vacancy. We share our sorrow with friends and with You, our God – hear now our silent sorrow.

Grateful, yes grateful, hear our gratitude for Betty –
for her dignity and integrity and gentle persuasiveness
and goodness –
grateful that she was so proudly herself,
yet treasured uniqueness in all people;
grateful that her faith was so real, so strong, so practical, grateful
that she felt for the blind so that they might feel
and see and be in touch.
That brotherhood and justice and peace
were for her living religion
and are her heritage and gift to us.

Support and strengthen all who love her, most especially, her family and those who needed her most…
Grant them a new and needed strength that life –
her life may go on,

on earth as in heaven.
We pray in triumph.
Triumph because of her life, its duration of three score years and
ten, its eternal implications in her children and grandchildren and
generations yet unborn;
in lives liberated and strengthened and opened
and supported and made better because of what she did and said
and was and is.
Triumph because love does lie over and around us
from our birth because there are friends on earth
and friends above.
Triumph because of You, Your creation and providence and redemption and victory alive to us in Jesus Christ. Help us to believe
and trust in the communion of saints, the forgiveness of sins, the
resurrection to life,
Christ's triumph as ours.
Oh God, make of these days and of this day
a day of promise,
of Christ's promise finally felt
and forever believed in the conviction
that death is not the last word,
that Christ is greater than the grave,
that his promise can be completely trusted.
A day of our promise not to forget,
but to resolve that we shall honor her example
in living and loving, and caring and helping,
in working for justice and peace
in the patient practice of her faith.
Amen.

Betty Klein

GORDON MAHY

GORDON MAHY was a tall man with a handsome, kind face and a loving spirit. With that bold shock of snowy white hair and mustache, he was our "great white father" and trusted friend. Each year at the last senior dinner, Gordon would compose a comic poem using the name of every single person in the graduating class. As those classes grew larger and larger, he depended on others to help feed him the necessary information to illuminate truths and details of the lives he honored. The poem was clever and eagerly anticipated and often hilarious.

Gordon had many talents and a plethora of interests – gardening and bird watching were two of his favorite ways to fill his days. Their front yard was a cornfield, and birds flocked to his feeders. After he retired, he happily volunteered in the campus garden. It was always enjoyable to be invited to the Mahy house to hear their stories. The ones about China were the best – filled with intrigue and narrow escapes. We marveled at the life they had led before coming back to teach English at WWC and were awed by all they had accomplished. They had been at Warren Wilson in earlier years, when they had to leave China during the war.

There is a great story about Eleanor Roosevelt visiting the campus at the end of World War II (March 1945), when food was scarce. The Mahy family lived in Dodge House and raised chickens. Something special needed to be served the great first lady, and Gordon offered his chickens. Kathrine Laursen prepared them carefully, and with her marvelous rolls and tasty vegetables, they used the best linen, polished the knives and forks to gleaming, and fed the whole community a grand wartime feast.

They Faithfully Led the Way

On a personal note, we discovered that Gordon's wife, Helen, a grandchild, Elora, and Fred were all born on September 23rd – so each year we had a three-cake birthday party, rotating locations. We got to know the Mahy family very well. Gordon and Helen birthed four children. They raised five, accepting as their own a daughter of Helen's sister who, along with her husband, had been beheaded by the Japanese while missionaries in China. A servant gave his life to spare their baby daughter.

Gordon and Helen had many talents, but their best one was their loving, embracing nature that encompassed all they knew.

In honor of Gordon while he was still teaching at Warren Wilson, Fred wrote a "senior poem" about him. Here is a portion of it:

Once upon a midnight bleary, while I pondered, weak and weary
on how to put it, what to say, of our senior, Gordon Mahy –
while I nodded, nearly napping, suddenly there came a tapping,
as of someone gently rapping, rapping at my kitchen door.
"'Tis some visitor," I muttered, "tapping on my kitchen door."
Quoth the OWL, "Nevermore…"

He said to me (in prose),
"We the ravens, sparrows, windhovers, owls
only speak to a very few –
      to the small man of Assisi in the brown cloak,
      to the tall man of Swannanoa with the silver halo.
As for you – you're on your own."

George Gordon Mahy is not a rich man, as the world measures wealth.
He lives comfortably but modestly.
You'd hardly call the car he drives a Rolls
and I don't think he has a closet full of Gucci loafers or Brooks Brothers suits.
If he did, he'd give most of them away, and the one he'd keep would

be well worn, used to work, and sooner or later marvelously rumpled and adorned with some of God's good earth.

But Gordon is wealthy. He may be the richest man I've ever known…
Rich in having chosen and having been chosen by his wife of nearly fifty years – Helen, dear, who first, last, and all ways has shared, supported and strengthened him.

Rich in where he's been and what he's done –
fording rough creeks and traveling long miles in the Kentucky mountains to preach the gospel;
compassionate missionary in China,
inspiring teacher in the Philippines and here,
poet, pastor, preacher,
man of prayer, lifting up to God words of beauty and grace,
words as true, as sweet, as honest as the man.

Rich in treasures who are his children and his grandchildren.
And, who has a larger family – extended, enlarging – all over the world.
A little girl who held his hand walking down a road,
a young man who never had a father until Gordon cared,
a lonely man whom he befriended – never judging, always patient,
a shy and sheltered student who came to study literature in one of his classes, and learned literature
and life
and loving.

FRED SPOKE THESE WORDS IN 1988 AT GORDON'S SERVICE:

"The fullness of joy," said St. Julian, "is to behold God
in everything."
Gordon Mahy was joyful for he did so many things well,
saw so many ways clearly,
was in touch with God in everything he was.
Gordon was rooted in God's good earth.
It was under his nails, on his clothes, under his feet,
and deep in his soul.
In compost and seedling, flower and fruit, in mushroom and in
sunflower,
Gordon enjoyed God.
These beautiful flowers in the chancel were grown by him.
Gordon also took flight with his beloved birds,
soared high above with Gerald Manley Hopkins,
Robert Browning,
William Wordsworth,
in his love of literature, journeys of the imagination and the spirit,
his transcendent affection for spring, nature, life, spirit, grace.
The beautiful memories in the chancel were also grown by him.
He forded rough creeks,
traveled long miles on horseback in Kentucky to preach the gospel.
He was a missionary in the best and truest sense,
winsome, never coercive
in Kentucky, in China, in the Philippines, North Carolina.
Pastor, poet,
professor in every sense of that word,
ornithologist, gardener, singer,
a loving and endearing husband to dear, strong, faithful Helen,
who was his love and his friend,
a great father to his children, a grandfather to eleven
grandchildren,
and hundreds of students.
His was a trusting soul, sometimes too trusting perhaps,

but he always gave people the benefit of the doubt, or rather of his belief.

I see him holding a little girl's hand on a path in a photograph I can never forget.

I hear him, that resonant, clear, compelling voice,

praying, singing, greeting you at the market.

His stature, face, presence are palpable.

He was liked – and more – he was respected –

and most – he was loved – how much, by how many, how clearly,

Gordon was loved.

He was such a good, good man, the best, and the very soul of this place.

He was as each of us knew him
he was as he knew himself
he was as he was fully known by God
and now he knows as he is known
his pain is over
his love fulfilled
and we rejoice!

* * * * *

This is how faculty member **Bill Mosher**, *who taught English and international studies, remembers Gordon:*

"Gordon Mahy – 'Dr. Mahy' to me as a young new teacher – was a revered figure and the reason that both I and Sam Scoville came to Warren Wilson. Our fathers both knew him. My own father had been a missionary in India and Gordon's brother-in-law, a missionary doctor, had taken out my little brother's appendix barely in time. So our families knew each other. He was guest preacher at his son-in-law's church in Ithaca, New York, where I was interviewing to teach 5th grade in a reform school. He invited me to come to Warren Wilson.

Gordon had been everywhere: a missionary in China, twice having to leave, once because of World War II and the second time when the communists under Mao Tse-tung took over. He had been a minister in Kentucky during the war and had taught briefly at Warren Wilson before coming back to teach again and then retire here. He bridged the Farm School and modern Warren Wilson College. We team-taught together, he taught poetry and I fiction, and little Lubie Cox handled composition for the whole college.

I was always in awe of him. He was such a kind and good person. His doctorate was honorary from somewhere, for the marvelous person he was. In the classroom it was his presence and person that was important. But I remember him more out of the classroom – where he was a thoughtful and considerate person in faculty meetings, a wonderful gardener who volunteered in the Warren Wilson Garden and filled his front yard with tall sweet corn amid all the other green lawns on College View Drive… a bird lover who led morning walks, who'd collect dead birds that we'd find and freeze until he could stuff and mount them in a case in Jensen (where Ann Turkle, later in fun, had knitted sweaters for them), a man who sometimes led services in twice-weekly morning chapel."

Christine Laporte Gardiner, *who is a gardener and nature lover herself, remembers this:*

"I was fortunate enough to meet Dr. Mahy in one of his (and my) favorite places at WWC – the garden. His passion for life on earth was evident in his interactions with students and in his actions during his leisure time: namely, gardening and birdwatching. As a member of the first summer garden crew in 1981, I was blessed with his example and insights about gardening, its relationship to wildlife, and the joys of creating a new fruitful and special place on campus.

I recall his gracious way of sharing his vast knowledge through little chats about the best way to scatter spinach seeds, or what sorts of flowers attracted one of our shared favorite bird species – goldfinches. Though I never had him as a formal teacher, he stands tall in my field of gardening mentors, passing the time together as he worked in his community garden plot, and I worked (with Ian Robertson and our crew) to establish the herb circle surrounded by boxwoods in a former pig field.

To this day, I think of him whenever I see a goldfinch alighting, like a bright idea, to feed on a flower that I have planted. Thank you, Dr. Mahy."

HELEN MAHY

FROM HELEN'S SERVICE IN 2001:

We are here, Lord, to remember, honor and celebrate
Helen Scott Mahy:
Christian, woman, sister, wife, mother, grandmother,
great-grandmother, missionary, leader, reader, writer, friend.
"Helen dear," Gordon called her, and Helen
              dear,
                    she was.
Vivacious, loving, intelligent, hospitable, dramatic,
of good courage and faithful service,
her frame diminutive, her soul so expansive,
an indomitable will wed to a sweet, sweet spirit,
and (ah!),
sometimes that impish, nicely naughty spirit
disguised in seeming naiveté!
She was uniquely herself and Your gift to us all.

Dear God, what a beautifully balanced team she and Gordon
made.
She not only believed in the priesthood of all believers, she lived
it.
She was an associate minister serving alongside Gordon in all their
joint pastorates.

We can still see in our soul's eye, the two of them together, Gordon lighting a fire in the fireplace on cold mornings, which she so enjoyed.
And when Gordon was dying, she read to him each day as was their custom – a good thing then, a good thing to do in childhood,

and something we all ought to do.

How proud she was of her children — each uniquely his and her
own person — testimonies to her skill in mothering.
How proud she was of all the children that You created through
them.

Thank You, Lord, for dear Helen.
We are grateful that she who knew the tragedy of a sister's mar-
tyrdom and the ultimate sorrow of outliving a son, also knew the
peace of a life, long and well — lived,
and the comfort, in the last six months, of being mothered at
home
by Gwen and her family.

Be, we pray, very present with her family gathered here and far,
and with all of us who shared with her —
deaths and births and birthdays,
loss and triumph, grace and blessing and... LIFE.
We shall miss her very much, but we do not grieve,
because she was who she was and because You... ARE!

We rejoice that she no longer sees through a glass darkly,
but face to Face;
that now and forever, she knows as she is known.
Hear our words and songs and sighs too deep for either.

Hear our praying,
    in Christ's good name,
                Amen.

Gordon and Helen Mahy

JAMES McCLURE CLARKE

JAMIE and ELSPIE CLARKE were singularly and together most exceptional people. Hickory Nut Gap, that old stage coach stop where they lived, was and still is one of those extraordinary places on earth that make you think all's well with the world. Boxwood and flowers and fruit trees and stables and animals and vegetable gardens and fields of green grass surrounded the old and oh-so-charming structure. Our children were always welcome to ride horses, and Elspie was a willing and dedicated teacher.

On Sundays there was hymn sing, and Warren Wilson students were welcomed home there. At Christmas the voices were accompanied by violins, and instrumental notes resounded in the bedecked rooms filled with smiling, delighted faces. There were picnics and square dancing in the summer, and that large oval blue and white-checkered table hosted the famous, the infamous and the ordinary folk all with the same courtesy and hospitality.

When Jamie was assistant to the president (1969-81) and later a trustee, the campus was the recipient of the Clarkes' sharing kindness in many forms. Many baskets of apples and gallons of cider nourished campus events. When he ran for Congress, we at the college all campaigned for our friend and rejoiced when he won – and Mr. Clarke went to Washington! There was so much going on in their lives that you wondered however it all got done. Everyone always forgave them when they were late. What a delightful way they found to live.

FROM HIS 1999 SERVICE:

A PRAYER OF THANKSGIVING FOR JAMIE:

Dear Lord, our God,
we call him "by his old familiar name." We remember Jamie and
celebrate all he did and everything he was. You graced his life
with bounty; he lived his life with quiet, faithful stewardship and,
oh, such generosity. We remember a gentle man, a man of courtesy, the delighted farmer, the husband in love, the beloved father,
grand father, great grand father. We rejoice that Mr. Clarke *did*
go to Washington (in an old pickup truck) and really represent
the people, standing up to injustice and standing up *for* ordinary
people in an extraordinary way because, for Jamie, there were no
"little people."

We remember him as a man of conviction and a real competitor
(any of us who ever saw him play basketball in his gym with his
boys could ever doubt that), but he was always fair and honorable.
He knew, Lord, how to win and how to lose. He reminded us that
there are worse fates than defeat and better destinies than victory.
Because he followed Christ and trusted You, he knew, like Paul,
how to accept both success *and* failure, every joy and even the unthinkable deaths of two of his sons.

We celebrate, O God, that Jamie "pursued peace with everyone,"
that he "lived in the light" and stubbornly refused to invite hatred
into the inn of his soul. Like love, Jamie was not boastful or arrogant or rude; like love, he was patient and kind and powerfully
modest. In a world where arrogance struts and preens, in a culture
where false modesty is all about in those who are so proud that
they are so very (h)"umble," we honor a *truly* modest man and who
of us cannot at this very moment see Jamie, slightly bent and looking down and offering out his hand, a man of authentic humility,
a *"genuine man,"* as one friend described him.

God of good hope, we do not despair. Jamie lived long and deeply and in good faith. He died *at home*... at home in his bed, at home on his farm, at home in our hearts. But he leaves, along with his legacy, a great *vacancy*. And so we pray, most especially, for Elspie, his partner, his friend, his love. Help her to grieve and not try to be *too* strong; help us to be there for her. We pray for Jamie's sons and daughters, whose tears are testament to the depth of their loss *and* the power of his love. We pray for *all* his children and his counted friends and for our own solitary selves.

Dear God, how often we take for granted and cut ourselves off and just don't get it... until we reach out and touch the strong and delicate web of life and see all the connections, an "absolutely un-broken continuity." We shake Jamie's gentle hand and we are, once again, in *touch* with Hickory Nut Gap and the South Pacific, with apples and horses, children and presidents, square dancing and pic-nics, streams of visitors from Fairview or halfway around the world and adopted children coming and going to that inn on the hill that is always open, that hospice, that home that is a *church* as surely as any cathedral, where everyone feels well come, where love is pal-pable, where family values like inclusion, love, joy, justice, hymn-singing and peace-making are said and sung, danced and lived.

Thank You, God, for Your great good gift of Jamie Clarke to us all. Thank You, that we *are* related, that we are alive in this awe-full, beauty-full world, that (who can believe it?) we are *at all*! Thank You, God, for EVERYTHING. Not everything is good, but all *is* well!

And now, as we say the old, familiar words of the Lord's Prayer, enable us to *pray* it together with *all* the saints:

Our Father who art in heaven, hallowed be thy name. Thy kingdom come, thy will be done, on earth as it is in heaven. Give us this day our daily bread; and forgive us our debts, as we forgive our debtors; and lead us not into temptation, but deliver us from evil. For Thine is the kingdom and the power and the glory, for-ever. Amen.

Jamie Clarke

ELSPETH CLARKE

FRED HONORED HER IN HER SERVICE IN 2001:

Thanks to You, Lord...
Elspie –
Like no other, one–in–a–universe,
to whom so much was given,
who gave so much more than ever was required.
We remember and we celebrate her, thanks to You.
Our thanks to You for her.

How seamlessly she integrated her public and private lives,
her world and her home, her work and her being,
all she did and who she so singularly was.
Who can believe all that she did?
She served in the Navy, as a member of "the greatest generation."
She was a wife who was also her husband's counselor and faithful
partner, the mother and anchor of eight children;
she planted, pruned, supported, helped, prayed, sang, campaigned
– she nurtured her family, good causes, vegetables, horses and
cows, chickens, apple trees, persons –
doing the heavy lifting and the unconditional loving –
and in her spare time – she took a breath.
Her wisdom, perception, and sophistication were disguised
in an old red checkered blouse, a slip that sometimes showed and
the cloud from a corn cob pipe.
She did it all with grace and courage and great good spirit,
for the faith which made her sing also lifted her up to You
through the excruciating losses of her sons and her husband.

We are most especially grateful, Lord, for the home she hosted.

We celebrate Hickory Nut Gap, where there was always room at the inn
that never ceased to be The Inn;
where the doors were always open –
to a politician from D.C. or a woman from up the valley, to students from around the world, to children learning to ride horses, to the rich and the poor, to those from Biltmore Forest or Sherwood Forest, open to pot lucks, picnics and square dances, democratic shindigs, football games, receptions, Christmas sing-alongs, weddings, children, cats and dogs and – JOY.

That place, whose very life Elspie hosted, should be on the International Register of Grace–Full Places.

We marvel, Lord, at all the lives she has touched, changed, made richer.
Hers was "a wonder–full life," and to imagine how it would have been and how it will be *without* her is <u>un</u>imaginable.

Near the end, when asked how she was, she spared her friends, because she was, in Mimi Cecil's words, a member of the "Fine, thank you, generation."   <u>Fine</u>, indeed! …And we thank You that she died, as did her beloved Jamie, in their own bed at their own home, encircled by her family, accompanied by the good old hymns and good-byes and love.

We pray for her family, her children, grandchildren, great-grand-children, extended family, for whom her absence is stunning. We are grateful that for them and for us all, her presence will be *palpable* at the Inn, in the county, around the world and in our hearts in an unbroken circle. And at the last, we rejoice with all our hearts that "Granny" and her best friend, "Grandy," and Mark and Bobo and old friends and new friends and all the saints are at home with You,
through Jesus Christ our Lord.
Amen.

Jamie and Elspie Clarke

JOAN DAY BEEBE

JOAN BEEBE was born and educated in New York — magna cum laude in music education from Ithaca College, further study in intercultural education at Columbia University, master's degree in rural sociology from Cornell — taught in Asheville for many years and championed good causes, trying to make a difference, especially in race relations. I always thought of her as a truly liberated woman who would go out on a very long limb to help anyone who needed help.

When David and Joan with their young daughter, Jane, joined the Warren Wilson community in 1961, Joan's first jobs were in the music department and teaching with Bill Klein in the social science department. However, by 1975, it was determined that her talents and skills were needed in administration. By 1981 she was the hardworking dean of the college, and her low-key, casual demeanor fit that leadership role very well.

"She was one of those people who did a lot behind the scenes; were it not for her creative thinking and quiet labor, much at WWC would never have come to be." **Terri Godfrey**, *who worked closely with Joan, remembers, "There she would be valiantly trudging off to a meeting with a stack of folders in her arms and a legal pad. I can still see her wonderful smile, hear her jolly laugh; remember her dry sense of humor. Joan had an uncanny knack for finding out the interesting, personal accomplishments of individuals and celebrating everyone's uniqueness, often pairing up people skills and integrating disciplines."*

Joan was extremely intelligent, and had so many talents and creative ideas, not the least of which was grant writing. In her proposals she used words well and secured millions for the college. **Sam Scoville**, *English professor and former dean, remembers Joan this way: "We made* *a great team — she as my associate dean, because she loved to find the money and organize and distribute it, and I didn't."*

Joan's keen eye saw the merits in WWC hosting the MFA Program for Writers in its fledgling years — and the program, in recognition of this support, created the Joan Beebe Teaching Fellowship in her honor. She was a fine musician, playing cello with the Asheville Symphony for many years, in the pit for our college theater musicals, and accompanying many chapel musical events. She was instrumental in helping establish Music in the Mountains (now Swannanoa Chamber Music Festival). She taught piano to campus children, using her talents freely wherever needed.

*She was gifted in so many ways, always kindly sharing with others. As French professor and later dean **Virginia McKinley** said of her, "In her gentle way, she made this whole place work… It is my hope that by her courage and by her encouragement, we have learned to encourage ourselves and each other. It is my hope that Joan has taught us all something about caring for each other…"*

FRED OPENED HER SERVICE in 1986 WITH THESE WORDS:

We are here because Joan Beebe died. We bring our sorrow because we loved her, because she was so present among us, because we can't really quite believe it. We come that our distress may be sanctified, our gratitude expressed, our faith strengthened, facing death and resurrection after Thanksgiving and before Birth. We come to remember Joan and to worship God. Let us do so in spirit and in truth.

PRAYER:

God of Grace, whose holiness elicits our humility,
whose mercy evokes our thanksgiving,

whose grace creates us each − different, special, unique…
and carries us all from beginning to end to re–birth,
whose grace is wiser than our ignorance,
more relentless than our willfulness,
and deeper than our un-knowing.
You have brought us here − together − in time
and led Joan home to eternity.
Receive our words and our music, hear our prayers;
enable us to honor Your Grace.
Amen.

AFTER A TIME OF SHARING, FRED PRAYED:

Thank You, God
For harvest and bounty, life and death, for everything
and for Joan −
his wife, her mother, their sister and our friend.
We recall with gratitude her searching mind,
great heart,   large soul,   real faith;
her love of music, her rage at injustice,
her organizational gifts,
her conviction,   compassion,   courage,
her liberalism in politics, in spirit,
in the time she gave to integrate a city,
or guide a frightened freshman,
in her unwillingness to "stay put" or "in place" −
oh, how she crossed lines, escaped boxes,
liked people from everywhere,   and every what,   and every who,
as the rainbow of her friends attests.
Each of us saw her from our perspective,
in as many different ways as we are people.
She was all of these; she is more of these.

How much she suffered this last year, with no self-pity,
and great, great will − faith − courage.
We are glad that her illness, her pain, her suffering are over.

We pray for her family – for David and Jane,
who depended on her for so much,
who will need each other more than ever... and us.
Help us to respect their privacy
and share their loneliness
and bless You
for Your gift of Joan to us,
now with the countless host,
still urging us on.
Amen.

*   *   *   *   *

These are **Larry Adamson's** *remembrances of Joan:*

"I think about Joan and her huge heart, concern for others, and brilliant mind. She was a wonderful spouse, mother and friend, a close friend to many of us. So easy to know, she had such a wealth of information to share. Her sensitivity to others, particularly her work with WWC students in sociology and social work, was very positive. The majority of our students were interested in that field then – and one reason was the focus of the college and the influence of Art Bannerman, Henry Jensen, Fred Ohler and Joan Beebe in guiding all of us.

Joan was a very supportive teacher and influenced students to 'do for others.' It was not only her class material, but the way she led her life and related to others which made such a wonderful impact on WWC students. I am a better person with more empathy because of such friends.

I knew her also as a gifted musician, playing the piano, organ and cello beautifully – as principal cello in the Asheville Symphony (we drove together with Fred and others to rehearsals), as a piano and organ accompanist (she was one of the best accompanists

I ever had when singing), as a piano teacher (her influence opened musical doors for my children, for which I am eternally grateful).

Joan was one of the brightest people I have known. She read avidly, had a very broad and deep knowledge. We had left WWC to return to Texas prior to her being dean of the college, but on several visits I was able to spend some time with her, and realized her sensitivity in guiding curriculum and supporting faculty as the dean. She was very well respected on campus and in the broader community. Joan was so sensitive to others. She was a liberal's liberal in the best sense of the word. I learned so much from her and will be eternally grateful for the experience."

Joan Beebe

MARTHA ELLISON

The college library was named for MARTHA ELLISON. She was head librarian when it was located in the log building that is now the print shop and work program office, and she was in charge of the operation to move to the new location. Martha was a gracious, gentle woman who never married, whose work was very important to her. She set her standards high and was excellent in her field. She was a dedicated church woman, holding the office of elder, and was respected by all who knew her. Normally, at most colleges, buildings are named for the donors who fund the buildings instead of the people who toil inside. Everyone on campus was very happy when the library was named for her. It was a classic Warren Wilson moment. She very much deserved the honor.

IT WAS 1984 WHEN FRED SPOKE THESE WORDS AT HER MEMORIAL:

"The world of books is the most remarkable creation of humanity. Nothing else that we build ever lasts. Monuments fall, nations perish; civilizations grow old and die out; and, after an era of darkness, new races build on others. But in the world of books are volumes that have seen this happen again and again, and yet live on, still young, still as fresh as the day they were written, still telling our hearts of the hearts of the centuries dead."

Clarence Day

"Books are masters who instruct us without rods, without words or anger, without bread or money. If you approach them, they are not asleep; if you seek them, they do not hide; if you blunder, they do not scold; if you are ignorant, they do not laugh at you."

Richard DeBury

We are here today to worship God and to give Him thanks for
Martha Louise Ellison,
reporter, librarian, archivist, builder, elder, clerk,
a woman of books,
a gentle woman of Christ,
and our friend.

She instructed us without rods, without words or anger, bread or
money.
When you approached her, she was not asleep.
If you sought her, she did not hide.
When you blundered, she did not scold;
and when you were ignorant, she never laughed at you,
but pointed you to truth's treasure…

Good God, we shall miss her —
her dearest friend, her family,
all of us who knew and respected and loved her
shall miss her very much…
but we cannot, will not, do not grieve
for hers was a peaceful and blessed death,
for her the busy world is hushed
and the fever and phantoms of life is over
and the work is done.

We do not grieve, because near the end she saw a vision of You —
And because she was a good and gentle woman of faith
who trusted the promises of Christ and lived what she believed.

We remember Martha and we are grateful
for her quiet, persistent, conscientious integrity —
for her fidelity to the church, visible and invisible
and to the Church's Lord;
for her vision, administrative skills and patience

that so fairly and wisely built the treasure of books
in the library that bears her name.
We honor her and all librarians who love the truth,
who urge us to stretch beyond our certainties and specialties,
our compartments and departments;
who fight censorship and the fear of new or disturbing ideas,
who keep long hours,
who relentlessly search out hidden answers to obscure questions,
who persistently sort through old books and dead minister's libraries
lest any treasure be lost,
who order, sort classify and enable the searcher
to find the heritage to be saved, the future to have a chance,
and wisdom to be served.

Be, O Lord, especially, deeply, clearly present with Mary,
with whom Martha never ever had an argument,
and fill the awe-full void in her heart.
Be, O Lord, especially, deeply, clearly present with her family –
with us all and with each
so that, in Your mercy, You may grant us, with Martha, a safe lodging,
and a holy rest, and peace at the last through Jesus Christ our Lord.
Amen.

Martha Ellison

VIRGINIA RATH

She was christened VIRGINIA RATH, but few knew her by that name. She was "Dinny," and as delightful as that name implies. Dinny had retired early from a long career in physical education at Swarthmore College when she came to Warren Wilson in 1965 as housemother at Sage. It wasn't long before other duties were asked of her, and she cheerfully complied. Those duties included being in charge of the newly added service component of the Warren Wilson triad although it wasn't referred to as the "triad" then. Because Dinny was service personified, it was logical that she should be involved in this crucial part of Warren Wilson.

Her enormous energy enabled her to step into many roles through her long life. Her two sisters joined her, and they built a house together on College View Road. Soon she had them participating in college life almost as actively as she did, though no one could keep up with Dinny Rath (pronounced the German way, "ROT.")

The Rath sisters were really something! I picture them singing or dancing together at so many campus functions. They loved to entertain and were quite talented in so many ways. I see Dinny with her violin – off to play in the Asheville Symphony, in the pit for a Warren Wilson musical or to an event in the chapel, I hear the three sisters harmonizing at a festival event, and Dinny dancing the Charleston in" The '76 Spectacular." She was a doer, and inevitably had everybody around her doing, too.

Fred knew her very well and captured her perfectly in what he said at her memorial service when she died at age 97.

FROM HER 1991 SERVICE:

Oh God, Your welcoming committee must have pulled out all

the stops for this newcomer! Are there brass bands in Your heavenly kingdom? You tell us of choruses of great praise, but are there balloons and great long streamers, colorful confetti and ticker tape? If I might make a suggestion, Dinny Rath's welcome home should be so happy and exuberant that we might hear it here on earth. And if You could whip up some snow, some skis or, lacking that, just some cardboard sleds or garbage can lids, she'll have all Your saints out there having a rollicking good time sliding down hills like delighted, transported children… in heaven, as it was… on earth."

We can see, in our imagination's eye, Dinny as a little girl, a "Pilgrim at Tinker Creek," with the whole Hollins campus as her heritage and her playground. We can see her at Swarthmore – teacher, archer, athlete, role model for generations of young women. We see her arriving at Warren Wilson, a Sage housemother, a mentor to so many students, teaching church school, serving her beloved church, coordinating and inspiring service projects, a coach, a scout leader, a ring leader, a cheerleader, like Mary Martin playing Peter Pan, " at play in the fields of the Lord."

We see her, good steward of her environment, bent over and cleaning up the trash from the sides of our roads in fair weather and foul, long before it was stylish or ever you got your name on a sign for doing it. We taste her homemade elderberry wine, which, if it didn't blow up in the fermenting of it, wasn't bad. We follow her on her Sunday-after church-hikes-up the mountain, trailing behind the students (50 years younger than she) who are breathless in her wake. We cheer for her as she wins gold medals in statewide competition in her late eighties. We are present once more in the home on the hill and there are Dinny and Gachu and Luise lighting the real candles on the great Christmas tree and we "ooh and ahh" and are nervous a lot that there might be too *much* splendor and we might behold, on that holy ground, the burning tree. We watch her dance the Charleston at a festival, hear her singing German songs with her sisters at an Oktoberfest, hear her and Gachu and Rodney Lytle sing the good old hymns at the bedside at Highland Farms.

Thank You, God, for Your gift of Dinny Rath to all our lives. She was a traditionalist *and* a rebel, a Christian in her time and a feminist before her time, an example of how to live and *why* to live. All her life she was good and strong and serving. And when she couldn't carry all that weight forever, she also learned, by Your Grace, to *be* – flawed and weak and helped.

We pray for her great-niece, her great-nephews, for *all* her children and sisters and brothers gathered here today, in the flesh and in the Spirit, around the world, *beyond* the world. We don't mourn… she lived long and beautifully, died peacefully, kept the Faith, made a difference, and is still a vibrant presence. If it is true that, at the end, we don't so much regret the things we *did* as the things we did *not* do, *not* dare, didn't have the courage or the faith to try, then our dear Dinny has *no regrets*. Even if she had only lived *twenty*-seven years instead of ninety-seven, she would have lived a long life because she lived so fully; at the end, she was still young.

In a world of "on the one hand, on the other," she believed fervently and never waffled. Amid all the hemmers and hawers, the scared and the safe, she took her stand and dared to be wrong. She did good; she did well; she made mistakes. But even when, occasionally, she played out of tune, she played boldly and passionately and with a grin on her face and she *never* played it safe.

She was *game*. She was a *player*. She played sports, fiercely competing to best *herself*. She played music *con brio*. She played her part at every stage with all her soul. She was gloriously at home in *all* Your fields – with flair and risk and great good gusto.

Dear God, it was,
  it *is*,
    it *will be*
our pleasure to *be* in her company.
Hear our words, we pray…

and the Word beneath the words…
    and the sighs too *deep* for words…
and hear us as we pray together the Lord's prayer…
Amen.

* * * * *

Alumna **Marion Yeager** *knew the Rath sisters well, and remembers when she was a student and spent time in their house:*

"I met Dinny Rath in 1986 or '87 when I was singing in the chapel choir. She and Gaku hired me to clean their house every Saturday morning. (This was after Louisa had passed). Their home had a comfortable deck with a spectacular view of the college farm and a variety of birds at the feeder. As I dusted and swept, they would follow me around the house and read to me. They enjoyed reading out loud to each other and to an "audience" (me). The book I remember most clearly was a history of the English language, but there were also stories and articles from *Reader's Digest*.

Dinny loved life. She had a very earthy sensibility. She chopped their fire wood; she was still skiing in the winter; she picked up trash along the roadside. Dinny made white wine from dandelion greens and red wine from elderberries. She was musical, theatrical, athletic. She was very direct and uncomplicated in speaking. She was clear about her opinions and confident in sharing them.

Dinny and Gaku adored their father. I heard many stories of their childhood in Virginia and their dad's German heritage and musical talent. At Christmas time, they decorated their tree with traditional German candles.

Dinny and Gaku had gone to college in the 1920s and become teachers. My grandmother was their age, had also gone to college that same decade and become a teacher. Whether they knew it or not, Dinny and Gaku became my stand-in grandmothers, and

I thoroughly enjoyed our Saturday mornings together. I believe both Dinny and Gaku (and Marian Anderson) performed on the WWC stage in the production of *The Duchess of Malfi*, which I stage managed. Dinny and Gaku were dynamic, engaging, and a delight to know.

My grandmother came to Swannanoa for my commencement. Dinny and Gaku graciously received my family (I believe there were eight of us) on their deck for an afternoon. I have a very sweet photo of my grandmother sitting outside with Dinny and Gaku."

Dinny Rath

HUGO DOOB

In 1967, HUGO and HILDA DOOB came to the campus later in their lives with so many talents to share. It was the right place for this marvelous couple, and they loved their life on the Warren Wilson campus.

Hugo was a New York native who had undergrad and Ph.D. degrees from Cornell, and he worked for years in chemical research. His skills were just what was needed in the Warren Wilson chemistry department which he expanded and enriched. I'm sure his WW salary was a fraction of what he earned before, but to him, life was about more than that. After he retired, he volunteered and came to the lab every day.

They were both so educated, Hugo and Hilda, so unassuming, so competent, and so right for our community. It was obvious they were happy being a part of Warren Wilson; you couldn't help but love them back. Hugo was a member of the American Guild of Organists and played frequently on the church organ. Hilda had many skills, among them the talent to make string puppets and perform them in lively puppet shows. She volunteered for most of our festivals to teach students and entertain the children with her wonderful little people.

The Doobs had such keen and searching minds and were great readers. On many an occasion Fred would get a note after a sermon, wanting to discuss issues he had raised. After Annette Schafer retired, Hilda was also Dr. Bannerman's very capable secretary. She lived a very long life and died recently in Massachusetts near her daughter.

FRED READ THIS IN THE CHAPEL ON A SUNDAY AFTERNOON IN OCTOBER, 1990:

Hugo Doob, Jr., died at home with Hilda by his side. Just a few weeks ago, he sent me the most recent revision of his wishes.

"There shall be no memorial service," he wrote. "People should be encouraged to pray wherever they might be — to pray for their own salvation and mine," he said. And then he suggested, if we wanted to, we might simply play the Brahms Requiem at the church and encourage people to come, to listen, to meditate, to stay as long as they wished. The Requiem will last 70 minutes.

The Brahms Requiem was then played, as people came and left. When it was over, Fred gave a benediction:

The grace of Jesus Christ,
the love of God
and the communion of the Holy Spirit be with you
this day
and forever.

Blessed are the dead
who die in the Lord from hence forth;
YES! says the Spirit,
that they may rest from their labors… and their works do
follow them. AMEN. *(Rev. 14:13)*

* * * * *

Hugo Doob was so unassuming and had such an impish look that it took a while before you realized just what a brilliant scientist, talented musician and learned man he was. **Dean Kahl** *tells us how much he taught him in the field of chemistry,* **Steve Williams** *attests to his fine musicianship, and* **Käthe Mosher** *says that he spoke German without a trace of an American accent. He was an extremely intelligent, gentle* *man, kind and giving, someone who practiced his beliefs.*

Dean Kahl, *WWC professor of chemistry, writes this about his old colleague: "Hugo was responsible for creating the four-year chemistry program at Warren Wilson. We still have a number of instruments that he ordered in 1968. Hugo was genuinely concerned about his students and worried about each one. A student who graduated from Warren Wilson in 1974 recently told me that much of his subsequent success was due to Hugo's influence."*

Hugo's body was given to science, and his ashes took a long time to come back to be buried. When they returned, Hilda wanted a grave-side service with the family. Knowing how Hugo disliked services or rituals, Fred was concerned about what to do, but agreed to go along with her wishes. Hugo and Hilda's daughter, a theologian, was to take part as well.

As the small group assembled around the grave, a large dog came from seemingly nowhere. In a strange way, the dog resembled Hugo. You know the way sometimes animals and their owners grow to look alike — well, this dog could have been Hugo's, although I don't believe the Doobs had a dog. He came right up to the spot where Fred was standing, stood in front of Fred, looked up at him and howled. He continued to howl and bark his displeasure until it was over. He left as quickly as he had come, disappearing into the woods. Hugo's daughter voiced the comment all were thinking. "Father did not like ceremony, did he?"

Hugo Doob

SAMUEL MILLAR

The Millars and the Ohlers were next-door neighbors for many years on the Warren Wilson campus. We were there for each other in good times and in difficult ones. The Millars were the very best neighbors anyone could hope for, and as I look back, the help and the joy they brought to our lives was incalculable.

When the buildings at UNCA were named for SAM MILLAR, the tributes to his tenure there were exuberant, but I remember best his years at Warren Wilson where his skills at his work and on the soccer field were beyond measure. Thankfully, as I put this book together, Helen is still participating in the WW church and being the same good friend to anyone who needs her. Sam's good deeds have been rightfully celebrated. Helen deserves the same praise and more for all she did and continues to do for our college and church community.

FRED'S PRAYER OF THANKSGIVING IN 1998 FOR SAM:

Thank You, God, for the gift of Samuel John Millar to us.
Sam was as each of us uniquely remembers him, as he saw himself,
the boy, the man, the public person, the solitary soul,
all of these and much more than the sum of them.
He was Your special human being,
and now he knows as he is known by You, and there is a glad reunion.
Thank You, God, for his presence, his fingerprints everywhere;
his courage, his will, and his wit.
Thank You for his passion, his love, his gregarious goodness, his tall soul.

They Faithfully Led the Way

What a long and fascinating pilgrimage he lived;
what an adventure now is his.

We remember with admiration that when the oncologist gave him
six months to live, he lived a year and a half, out of stubborn resolve "to show them,"
an indomitable spirit and humor's sense.
Thank You for the extra time – with all its pain and frustration,
it was a gift to help Helen finally face death,
to draw the family even closer together,
and to help us all to look back in gratitude, look within in honesty,
look ahead in faith.
Hear the thanks of a daughter who mothered her father at the end,
and of a son who talked to his father man to man.
Hear the thanks of Shannon, Samantha, Jennifer and Emily
for a grandfather's love.
Hear Helen's thanks for nearly half a century of providence,
adventure, and love.
She hurts so much because she loved so deeply.
We promise You that we will support and encourage her
so that she may,
in time, realize just how strong she truly is.

Thank You God, for all who helped along the way…
Helen most of all – for 48 years and that last, long night,
the nurses and doctors, neighbors, friends, family,
and especially, Patty and all the saints from Hospice who came,
and cared and enabled Sam to die at home
with his pain relieved and his dignity enhanced.
Dear God, enable us to affirm the life that overcomes death.
Lord of Life, live and sing and love in us.
In Christ's good name we pray.
Amen.

REMEMBERING SAM:

Samuel John Miller was born in 1924 in Belfast, Northern Ireland. He was raised in a Protestant, middle class home in a neighborhood rife with sectarian hatred. His father was a fierce Orangeman and dogmatic moralist, but Sam, even as a boy, saw further than his father. One of his pals was a ne'er-do-well and one of his best friends was Frankie Taggart, a Roman Catholic kid who grew up to become a Jesuit priest. Sam's mother died of pneumonia when he was only five years old, a blow which haunted him all his life. He was a fine athlete, excelling in rugby and football and a superior student.

Trained in Ireland as an engineer, Sam's first job was with the world famous Belfast shipbuilders, Harland and Wolf, which had built such great liners as the Olympic and the Titanic. He enlisted in the RAF and served with courage and distinction as a flight engineer in air/sea rescue serving in Egypt, Macao, Singapore and Hong Kong – where he met Helen Long, a Presbyterian missionary nurse who had served in China. Theirs was a short courtship and a long marriage, as good as it was sure.

In 1956, Sam, Helen, Georgena and Samuel immigrated to America, where Sam was immediately hired by Western Electric in New Jersey... then drawn by a deep call to service, they came to Warren Wilson College, where Sam was the campus engineer and soccer coach. He developed some great teams, regularly defeating Duke and Chapel Hill varsity teams, played in the nationals, fielding the only integrated team. A recognized leader among soccer referees, he initiated women's teams and did more than anyone in the area to pioneer the game of soccer.

Helen was a campus nurse, managed the bookstore, counseled and befriended countless students. They were both active in this church, Sam an elder and lay preacher. In 1971 Sam was hired by UNCA, where he reorganized and directed all engineering, maintenance and building. He coached soccer, worked hard, made friends.

Sam Millar was one of the first to greet and welcome Beverly and me when we returned in 1958. I've known him for almost 40 years. He was my close, very dear and my trusted friend. When our little daughter Lisa called him "Fah," for God-only-knows what reason, he has kept that name all his life. Fah was spirited and feisty, opinionated, funny, with a glow in his eye and a brogue in his voice.

He had a great work ethic, ever before that expression was coined. He was raised, as were many of us, in a rigid, judgmental Christian tradition. Unlike so many, he grew and learned; his world, his faith, his understanding of God expanded. There were spirited theological debates, many scrabble games and – theater. He loved to perform. While I was playing violin in the pit, Sam was Mr. Lundy in Brigadoon. Backstage in the dark he fell off a platform, tearing all the ligaments in his leg. Next night he insisted on performing with his cast made up to look as though Mr. Lundy had gout!

Sam would light up a room when he entered, and wherever you went with him, someone would always call out, "Hey, Sam!" He was one of those rare people like Ben Holden, who genuinely attracted and loved people. Sam and Helen were, to so many students, surrogate, substitute, NO – *real* parents for those with none (or worse). Just the other day, an alumna remembered Sam reading Dr. Suess his children and invited the students to listen when they visited.

I saw Sam – quite literally – come back from the dead twice, thanks to Helen and modern medicine and the grace of God. Always I saw him savor life, like good Guinness Stout, and drink deeply of it.

I shall never forget an unexpected, out-of-the-mundane, epiphany that happened one day. We and the Millars took a drive together on a Sunday afternoon. We were on a back road to Marion, nothing special on a very non-extraordinary day, when without warning or prelude, Sam cried out,

"I have this overwhelming feeling of... WELL BEING!"

So he did
　So, did we.
　　So, should we all.

Sam Millar

WILLIAM PENFOUND

How lucky Warren Wilson was in 1967 to welcome "Pen" – rarely called WILLIAM – and ELLEN PENFOUND to the campus. Tall and lanky, usually sporting a beret (often red) and jaunty bola ties, Pen was a botanist, fascinated and learned about all living things.

He'd wade in the Swannanoa River and identify everything in it. His classes were strict and demanding; he had no patience with tardiness or insubordination. Many a student's heel was bruised by the closing door, as they tried to rush into their seat before the bell rang.

Born on a farm, Pen went to Oberlin and got his Ph.D. from University of Illinois. He met Ellen at Iowa Teachers' College, where she taught English and botany as well. He was well over six feet tall. She – maybe 4 foot ten. Having lost a lung in a bout with tuberculosis, Pen was nevertheless able to keep up with her, hiking up Pike's Peak in Colorado, where she proposed to him.

They moved to the French Quarter, and he taught at Tulane for almost 20 years. After a time at the University of Oklahoma, they moved to Warren Wilson, where Pen energized the sciences, helping to create Warren Wilson College's Environmental Studies Department.

They gave over ten good years to WWC. After he retired, he still came back to give seminars and substitute. He made sure that when he died, part of his estate would be invested in a savings account given each year to a student majoring in environmental studies – which has become one of the most renowned departments of Warren Wilson.

FRED TOLD PEN'S STORY AND HONORED HIM AT HIS SERVICE IN 1984:

William Theodore Penfound was born, the 4th of 11 children, about 87 years ago in the Lorain Valley of Ohio, near Elyria, and grew up on the family farm. Five brothers and two sisters still live there. Pen was the one who left home – from Ohio to Illinois, Louisiana, Oklahoma, New York, Alabama, New Zealand, Australia and the Swannanoa Valley – always the explorer, the scientist, the seeker. But, in recent years, in his writing, "The Penfound Story," in the memories he shared each day with Ellen, and most recently, in the autobiography he had just begun – the very first sentence of which reads, so characteristically: "I changed from an aquatic animal to a terrestrial creature at about 2 a.m. on November 8, 1897…" Pen was returning to his origins, completing the circle, going home.

As I thought of his long, rich sojourn, and as I reread his description of his early life on the Penfound farm – as without water or electricity or modern plumbing, but as a place which was a world of togetherness where the kitchen was warm with home-baked food, and the sugar maple trees leading to the house – again in his words, "severely attractive in winter, especially when laden with snow" – I was reminded of a beautiful poem – "The Mist on the Mountain," by Loren Eiseley. Like Pen, a scientist, a clear thinker, a man of many parts and broad interests, a man of the spirit and the spirited, who also left the Midwest to search out the treasures of God's world, who late in his life turned toward home. And this is what he said:

"Through the night mist on the mountain
I see far away a light in a farmhouse window on the plain,
The mist mellowing it until it glows yellow as the kerosene
   lamps of my boyhood
By which I first studied, the lamp of home far away in the
   mist.

I travel down the rays like a homing insect
Beating the moth wings of thought until I stand by a drab
    house at the edge of town
Peering in, as through time, at a little window
At the oilcloth table
At my mother, my father, at myself
A child of five, reading a primer,
Mouthing the letters.
It snows, obscuring the lamp until, in a Great Plains blizzard,
I find myself in a self-constructed Eskimo igloo
Waiting with the family lantern in the yard,
For father to come up the path from work
Lift me and take me inside the house
To the warm flickering wicks
Before the harsh electric glare replaced them.
I remember sitting in the snow house waiting.
Time why did you run? Where is the polished brass lamp, the
    oilcloth,
Where is the warm oven with the isinglass windows
By which we dressed in the cold mornings
Where is the old farm bed in which I huddled with warm bricks
    at my feet?
Where are even the words of that time, some lost, no longer
    spoken by living men?
Father, mother, take me back even though life was harsh
In the small kitchen
Who would have dreamed
The universe so large? Through the mist on the mountain
I descend, beating the moth wings of thought
hovering before the window
watching an hour long vanished,
myself, who never grew up, but simply
disappeared with all the others.
Can there not be miniature time? Some place where one stays
Forever at the kitchen table,
On the same page of one's book,

With one's parents looking on,
An old photograph perhaps,
but that would have faded.
We would not truly be there.
In the night mist on the mountain I put out my hands
but the light was gone, a fog is descending,
I do not recognize this alien grownup body.
I will not recognize it ever,
I am there, there in the yellow light in the kitchen
Reading on the stained oilcloth.
We are all there. I did not grow up.
It is not I in the night mist on the mountain.
It is not I making these pained animal sounds,
Wrinkling my forehead.
I have rushed like a moth through time toward the light in the
     kitchen.
I am safe now, I never grew up.
I am no longer lost in the mist of the mountain.

Nothing is lost; there IS "miniature time" in the eternity of God;
and he who was changed from aquatic animal to terrestrial creature,
from boy to man, has rushed life like a moth through time
toward the light in the kitchen, to celestial being
home to the mind of God.

PRAYER:

Eternal God,
God of science, beauty, truth
present in a tiny flower or a flaming sun
yet more than they.
God of creation, order, redemption, return
God of forthrightness and plain speaking,
foe of all that is false

help us to speak the truth, honor our friend,
share our loss and our gratitude
bring to You our faith
our needs
each alone
all together
and accompanied by Christ
whose life and death reveal Your face,
who was and is Your great miracle
and great hope
our Savior and our friend.
In His unconquerable name we pray,
amen.

A PRAYER FOR PEN:

O God, before whom generations live and die,
we praise You for all Your servants who,
having lived this life in faith,
now live eternally with You.
Especially we thank You for Your servant William,
for the gift of his life,
for the grace You have given him,
for all in him that was good.
Like his father, he too was "an uncompromising foe of hypocrisy."
And we can still hear him cutting through the pretense, false piety,
shabby thinking, of others and sometimes of ourselves.
How he loved to argue, to battle for ideas, clearly, fairly.
Like his mother he loved music and reporting, and we remember
him smiling over his viola or chronicling a genealogy, a population
study,
a research paper, a view of this valley.
We can almost see the string tie, the backbone and the carriage –
that face that belonged on Rushmore
(but for the glimmer in his eye and the humor in his soul).

We can almost hear him say, as he did so often to his friend,
"Never felt better; had less."
And for his tough and gracious uncomplaint through all the later days,
we are grateful.
He was a master of so many tasks and a taskmaster,
but, he demanded most – most of all – of himself.
We thank You that for him, death is past and pain is ended,
and he has entered the joy You have prepared.
We pray for Ellen.
Be with her—in sighs too deep for words.
Be with her in her way and in Yours.
Be near their children and their grandchildren
and with his whole family and friends –
so that we who remain will continue Pen's story
and respect his good memory by being as fiercely,
authentically our own true selves – as he was.

God of grace, give us faith to see beyond touch and sight –
Your kingdom,
and where vision fails, help us to trust Your love, which never fails.
Honor and praise, now and forever,
Amen.

Pen Penfound

ELLEN PENFOUND

AT ELLEN'S SERVICE IN 1985, FRED PRAYED THIS:

We are here today to worship God, to witness the resurrection
and to remember and honor Ellen Armstrong Penfound –
mother, wife, sister, grandmother, great grandmother,
elder, activist, lover of nature and nature's God… and our friend.

We remember –
her strength of soul and will, clothed in that small, spare body.
We remember –
her spunk and spirit, the wit and humor and good grace
with which she lived so long and well,
with courage,
with caring for bird and river, citizenship and discipleship,
for friend and foe, family and stranger,
those she mothered or taught or befriended,
him whom she married.
Lord, she was Pen's match in mind and will and heart;
she stood up to him and beside him,
lived with him in sickness and in health,
his woman for all seasons –
and how they loved each other – wife and husband – and lovers
and peers, and friends.
They loved deeply and came so far together,
went to bed in memories to old stories at the end –
and now are met again in Your eternal future.
Her children and their children, her sisters and all her friends
rise up and call her blessed, and to theirs and our lives – a blessing.
We remember Ellen's great intelligence,
her sharp no-nonsense, perceptive mind –

even toward the end in her other conscientiousness,
the quickness, the relentless perceiving, the flow of ideas.
And we remember her before – the Wellesley girl, the mature woman;
we remember also that nothing is forgotten,
that You know every detail,
that like a genealogical aunt or
a great-grandfather with a photographical memory
You – take it all – take us all in
remembering for us when we forget, lose it, blot it out, can't recall.
And You do it, Oh God!
Not in relentless judgment with some cold, cruel, unblinking eye,
but with unremitting love so that nothing, nor no one should be lost –
not her birth in New Jersey, nor her death in Texas, nor anything in between.
And, at the end
each of us will see, with Ellen, our whole lives
and Your grace flash before us
and we will finally get it and know as we are known,
no longer through an imperfect dim pane,
but face to Face –
healed, whole, remembered, remembering
and radiant.
Amen.

HOWARD THOMAS

AT HOWARD "TOMMY" THOMAS'S SERVICE IN 1991, FRED REMEMBERED HIS LONG AND DISTINGUISHED CAREER MINISTERING AND TEACHING:

HOWARD THOMAS was born on September 11, 1906, to Cora and John Thomas in Byrnedale, Pennsylvania. He graduated from Wheaton College, received a divinity degree from McCormick Theological Seminary, and earned a master's and Ph.D. from Cornell. He was a pastor of churches in Illinois and North Carolina, as well as a missionary under the Presbyterian Board of Foreign Missions among lepers of the Tai-Lu people along the Burmese border in southwestern China, where he was appointed supervisor of the South China leper colonies.

Immediately following Japan's attack on Pearl Harbor, the Thomases were interned by the Japanese in Thailand until mid-1942. He helped to direct rural development for U.S. A.I.D. in Laos, was a professor at Colorado State and Cornell, then taught and chaired the department of sociology at Warren Wilson for many years. A member of many professional societies, he published numerous studies about leper colonies and migrant workers. He died at the age of 84.

We, his family and friends are here today to worship God and to honor Tommy. He lived a remarkable life in faith, he died at peace, he lives in us.

PRAYER:

We remember, O God, a man –

each of us from our own perspective and experience
from near, nearer, closest of all —
Dr. Thomas,
Howard,
Tommy.

We remember him for what he did and who he was.
We saw him in as many ways as we are people.
He was all of these,
he is more than these.
We are so grateful that throughout his long internship of dying,
he had such a sweet spirit,
he knew our faces.
We are most grateful that his long passage is over,
that now he knows as he is known,
that the perception, that incisive mind is back, and more!
We look back and see him still — the handsome face,
the beautiful smile,
the knowing look —
the scholar, the believer, the analyst, the participant,
the missionary, the learner.
Demanding/generous
stern/vulnerable
teaching his students — tending/attending his stunning roses
both blooming because of his knowledge and his love.

Be, O God, very near to all who loved and miss him —
most specially, be with dear Ruth,
most close, most bereft.
We do not ask You to take away her loneliness,
nor remove her sorrow,
as though Tommy's presence could be blotted out or time alone
heal.
You heal her —
take her loneliness near to Your heart —
which is Love —

which remembers and cries and sings.
Be present and real to Tommy's brothers, his sister,
his nieces and nephews, all his friends.

O God, You heard his constant, uncompleted prayer.
You completed it and took him home
to join that great company who have finished their course in faith.
Help us who remain behind
To believe, to dare, to live
from faith to faith
until the glad reunion
in Christ's powerful name we pray.
Amen.

* * * * *

Retired business professor **John Showalter** *remembers the Thomases:*

"We were neighbors on Rainbow Ridge. Tommy and Ruth were sociable folks, always had a nice departmental Christmas party at their house and were active on campus.

He often spoke of his years in Laos/Cambodia. There was a lot of intrigue in that part of the world back then, and he had developed a fondness for the Laotian people. If I recall correctly, he could speak the language. Students liked him; I think he came across as sort of a father figure to many. He was a good man who led our department well."

RUTH HATCHER THOMAS

RUTH THOMAS worked tirelessly alongside her husband throughout his life. She was also a Dr. (Dr. Ruth) and had been a Presbyterian missionary nurse in a rehabilitation program at the leper colonies in southwestern China, where she oversaw medical services and training. Like her husband, she too died in 1991.

THESE ARE FRED'S WORDS FROM HER MEMORIAL SERVICE:

PRAYER:

Thank You, Lord, for the unique, precious, like-no-other
gift of Ruth Thomas to the world –
to her family – to her friends – to us all.
What a treasure she was – how we treasure our memories of her.
She was clear proof that stature has nothing to do with size.
We recall her intelligence, her perception, a Dr. with no pretension,
wise without arrogance.
We celebrate all her graces – of manners and goodness and spirit.
She seemed never to judge others – as we so easily do,
never to condemn or envy or presume.
She was grateful for all Your blessings, gracious under pressure,
a woman of such quiet, authentic, decent courage.
Nurse, missionary, supervisor, professor, prisoner of war, maker of
peace, elder, hostess, friend, nurse to her beloved Tommy.
How gently, how patiently, how lovingly she stood by his side,
sat by his bed, spoke with sighs too deep for words
and the touch, the hands of love.

Thank You, God Almighty, that she is free at last, free of cancer,
free of pain, free of every limit this side of the door.
Thank You, God, that she has gone through the door to eternity
and glad reunion with her lover –
on to glory – full and fine and free.
That glory we glimpse.
Help us to see more and fear less,
to mean what we say and live what we hope,
that, further on, we too may be present
and accounted for with all the saints,
with Jesus Christ our Lord,
Amen.

* * * * *

Dennis and **Kay Stockdale** *remember the Thomases' kindness
in entertaining overseas students. As they recall: "They were noted
among the Middle Eastern students for hosting them for meals at their
house, even letting them use their kitchen to prepare their own special
recipes from home. Dr. and Mrs. Thomas would prepare a native meal
(authentic too; coffee with cardamom seeds, for example, invite a few
students and some faculty. We were invited and enjoyed one of those
meals. The students loved it. It gave them a chance to relax, unwind,
and enjoy one another in a way that did not happen on campus."*

*Overseas students, who rarely got to return home for vacation
breaks, especially looked forward to being in faculty homes. The Thomases, having lived out of the country for so much of their earlier life,
knew firsthand what it was like being away from home and far from
things familiar. They knew food was something that was missed most.
Such thoughtfulness exemplified them both.*

Tommy and Ruth Thomas

JOHN ABERNETHY

Among JOHN ABERNETHY's many claims to fame in a life full of accomplishment, he was the good mayor of Montreat. As a Presbyterian minister, when John and his charming wife, Jean, moved there, he had too much energy to retire, so in 1976 he joined the WWC staff as church relations director. In those years we were closely connected to the church and received much help from individual churches across the country and mission stations around the world. John's office secured that connection, and through it we received many students and much support. Both he and Jean were active participants in campus activities, were always eager to help with festivals, and were devoted members of the Warren Wilson Church. Tall, sandy-haired John and quick-witted Jean wore their Scots plaid with distinction, and were loved and respected by all who knew them.

AT JOHN'S SERVICE IN 1994, FRED PRAYED THESE WORDS:

Beneath "Your watchful care and tender mercies," Oh, Lord,
John was born, grew, learned,
became the special person You intended at his creation –
blessed by his parents, the Church, "his people" –
Proud to be a Scot, a Presbyterian, an Abernethy –
and therefore warmly ecumenical, genuinely inclusive…
A man whose race was human, whose politeness was respect,
whose manners were moral.
We marvel that he did so much –
that his life was one of service –
as a minister of the gospel, in service in the church,
in her courts and colleges,

in evangelism and the nurture of future ministers,
in Rotary, in all he did for Montreat,
in every way he served THIS special place,
where his gentleness and kindness were honored
and recognized as the strength they were.
We remember his quiet, stubborn struggles for racial justice
and human decency
and the un-bitter and gracious way
he met bigoted, nasty criticism
with a gentle spirit, and the startling blessing of meekness.

Within "Your watchful care and tender mercies," O Lord,
we thank You for our friend, John.
He did so much;
he was even more.
We would neither deny nor forget his moments of anger,
impatience, even occasional rage –
at injustice, at his withering powers.
But they were minor motifs in a life of such sweetness of spirit.
John was courteous and kind and sensitive
as few men are.
He really tried to live Christ's beatitudes,
and his humility, peace-making, turned cheek
and loving spirit blessed us all.

Embrace, O Lord, John's family, his children and grandchildren
in "Your watchful care and tender mercies."
They went with him on his long, last, difficult journey,
and it was, O God, like a pregnancy of travail and passage
and deep birth pangs.
His children were his midwives, and finally –
His pain transcended, every ounce of will and strength spent,
he was born into the brilliant and loving light of all Christ's eternity.
Who of us when we were earth-born, could imagine
that our passage would emerge into such a world as this?
Who of us could begin to appreciate the splendor of the nativity?

We suppose – he knows – and she –
and all of them who rest "from their labors."
Hear us, as we now join in their distant song of triumph –
"Beneath Your watchful care
and tender mercies."
Amen.

John and Jean Abernethy

HERBERT FITTON

HERB FITTON was educated at Harvard University. After a teaching career in Connecticut and New York, serving as a lieutenant commander in the U.S. Navy during WWII and director of the Veterans Administration Center at Harvard, he came to chair the department of mathematics at Warren Wilson in 1965. A man of many talents, at the senior dinner he often helped his friend, Gordon Mahy, write and deliver the senior poem in which all graduates were recognized.

Herb did an enormous amount of volunteer work in Asheville, and for his own pleasure he acted with ACT, Asheville Community Theater. That acting ability resulted in his being cast as Mr. McLaren in our own production of "Brigadoon." He performed beautifully in the run of that musical not long before he died. He was 75. He and his lovely wife, Polly, were active in all campus and chapel events and were a treasured addition to the community.

It was a most moving memorial service for Herb. When the choir – which had all performed in the same production together – sang songs from "Brigadoon" at his service, and the leading lady, Helen Woodruff (who played his daughter) sang a solo, the sobs were audible. Tight families are often forged while working together on such a play. Herb's dying had indeed become a death in a very large family. To me, the remembrance of his death will always be interwoven with our venture to that mysterious place in the Scottish Highlands.

**AFTER HERB'S FRIEND, GORDON MAHY, SPOKE
PERSONALLY ABOUT HIM AT HIS SERVICE IN 1979,
FRED SAID THESE WORDS BEFORE AND AFTER THE
CHOIR SANG:**

Another way of speaking of time, eternity and love
is in the word and music of an experience in which most of us
shared —
a real fantasy
hospitable and philanthropic and unforgettable
in which Herb took part
to which he contributed so much as Mr. McLaren
as poet of the event at the cast party
— as Herb —
Time, eternity, love — Brigadoon.
Why one hundred years is a day and a day can be eternal.
In the words of Brigadoon:
"Real loneliness in not loving and losing
Real loneliness is not being in love at all."
If you love someone deeply, anything is possible.

PRAYER:

Not a tear but a prayer?
Dear God, both tears and prayers — we offer them both —
Tears of sorrow, of sentiment, of joy, of gratitude, of love, of caring.
Forgive us all — our holding back and keeping in,
our fine distinctions and timid withdrawals.
More tears of sorrow and joy,
more caring, living, loving
in the face of every disguise death wears —
coldness — safety — isolation — sophistication
                    invulnerability
in the face of every cocoon.
More love, more deeply, more often.

Ohler

Our prayer is praise
    for Your love
        in the beginning, at the end and now
in Herb, in his 75 years
in Grandma Fitton and Polly and Nancy and Robert and David
    and their families
in his friends and neighbors
in all the web of life and death
and love –
possible
miraculous love
all around us.
Receive our simple gifts – tears – prayer – praise
in Christ's name and in the words he taught us.

BENEDICTION:

Go into time having glimpsed eternity.
Go into the warring world in peace – Christ's peace.
Be courageous, for though death is everywhere,
love is greater
and possible and miraculous
and anything and everything.
Love each another,
Amen.

Herb and Polly Fitton

WARREN WILSON HAMPE

"WARREN WILSON" HAMPE — yes, that was his actual chris-tened name — but we at Warren Wilson all knew him as "Pop." His daughter, Barbara, had come to teach history at the college when she was quite young, so he knew about the place for a very long time before he got personally involved. He was an insurance man most of his life, but when he retired he found he still had energy, and he always had a great sense of mission. He came to Warren Wilson in 1960 and be-came a recruiter, traveling to find students who would fit into Warren Wilson's way of life and learning. He was the college's first recruiter, and he brought us some very good students, some graduating in our first senior class.

While on campus, when he wasn't on the road he lived in St. Clair and kept a careful eye on his recruits. He cared deeply about them and was often seen on campus with a concerned expression on his face listening intently to a student's problems or questions. You always knew that Pop Hampe cared.

WHEN POP HAMPE DIED IN 1971, FRED PRAYED:

We remember, O God, a man —
each of us from his own perspective and experience —
near or nearer, years ago — last week,
as his child, his grandchild, brother, friend.
We saw him in so many different ways as we are people.
He was all of these.
We are glad that he is fully known by You — fully know and fully

loved.
We now, in silence, want to pray and to thank You for Warren
Hampe
and what he means to us.

We cannot long feel sorry because he lived as he did,
because he was who he was
a human being, a good man, a reconciler…
a man who really cared for people,
who struggled and didn't always find life easy
but rich and worthwhile and, O God, so full.
We thank You that he was thoughtful in little things –
like remembering birthdays, saying a kind word when you were
down,
being "gramma" to a little girl, and doing a thousand, thousand
things to make it better, fairer, kinder, than it would have been
without him.
We thank You that he was faithful in what matters most –
service, friendship, persistence, love, faith –
here and long before he came here.

We thank You for Pop – that he was father to his children and
grandchildren.
That he was Poppa to so many young men and women.
All his children remember
And say thank You.
What we owe him we cannot repay…
But we promise You – it will go on… to all generations.

And we cannot long feel sorry
because he believed You
he trusted You
he lived in faith and died and lives in faith.
He died living;
he would not have us live dying.
He would have us as befits Christians

to be of good cheer, and be the saints we are —
to go back to Your word,
do Your work, wherever we go, whatever we do.
We shall try.

After the service Fred received a letter from a family member that contained these words: "He left us a heritage of reconciliation, reaching out to all sorts of people, and an unwillingness to become bogged down in mean and petty things. I hope we can live up to that."

*　*　*　*　*

Alumnus, teacher, artist, director, former WW faculty member and artist-in-residence **John Koegel** *remembers Pop Hampe:*

"The 1965 snow that was falling on the bronze lions at the Art Institute of Chicago when I was a student there, was also falling in the mountains of Western Maryland. My parents had gone on that snowy evening to the First Presbyterian Church in Cumberland to hear about Warren Wilson College from Mr. Hampe, the college's representative and recruiter. My folks liked this jovial man and trusted that what he had to say about that small Presbyterian college in Swannanoa, North Carolina offered just the right things their 'arty' son was unaware he needed!

Anyway, Pop presented my folks with a fine college plan for me, and I couldn't defend my arty ways against the three of them. They were, after all, practical folk. When it came to answering, 'So what will you do with an art degree?' I had no answer. Of course, as an English major at WWC, the answer as to what I'd do with *that* degree was questionable, too. But in the fall of 1965 at Warren Wilson, I'd see Pop walking from St. Clair to his car with his suitcase in hand, readying for another recruiting sojourn. He'd become a kind of grandfather fellow to me by that time, always asking me about my folks, and how I was doing, too.

They Faithfully Led the Way

When I think back, I was at Warren Wilson in the time of the grandfathers – Dr. Mahy, 'Fessor' Laursen, Dr. Klein, Dr. Bannerman and dear Pop Hampe. We won't see the likes of them again, but how fortunate I was to have known such caring and honorable men. Their generosity of spirit was as significant to my getting along in the world as was any classroom course of study. And to think, I owe it all to Pop Hampe talkin' to my folks on a snowy evening..."

Pop Hampe

MICKEY
McCONNELL

When MICKEY MCCONNELL came to our campus in 1974 as a volunteer on Ben Holden's staff, my baseball-loving, former-coach-husband was overjoyed.   Mickey had an important and impressive career with Fred's favorite team, the Brooklyn Dodgers.   Fred was fascinated to hear the details of his work with Leo Durocher and Branch Rickey, signing players like Jackie Robinson, Joe Black, Junior Gilliam. In early years Mickey had been a sportswriter and broadcaster, doing a weekly show with Howard Cosell.   I think my husband was star struck and could not get enough of his stories.   After Mickey's 11 seasons with the Dodgers, he spent 25 years as training director of the International Little League and wrote five books on baseball.

His interests and concerns, however, were not only for baseball and sports; he truly cared and tried to make the world a better place.   He understood the dangers of environmental rape and nuclear buildup and spent decades as a moving force in Yokefellow Prison Ministry.   An active elder in the Presbyterian Church, he believed in our college and came to help in whatever way he could.

Ben tapped his talents in community and church relations and as advisory coach to the baseball team.   The McConnells were not campus residents for as long as most people in this book, but their contribution was significant and noteworthy.   In the last decade of their lives Mickey, with is lovely wife, Alice, were vital and dedicated members of the WWC community.

THIS IS PART OF FRED'S PRAYER WHEN THE MICK-EY McCONNELL BASEBALL FIELD WAS DEDICATED ON CAMPUS:

Lord of all life,
  we dedicate a field – a baseball field –
  a special place
  where the rules are fair, the limits are defined,
  where "the boys of summer" will play, win, lose,
  and learn what matters more than either, most of all.
  We dedicate this field to honor our friend, Mickey McConnell –
  gentle man, relentless advocate, coach, scout,
  believer in – You,
  in countless young people, in us.
  His life goes on – in this field, which now bears his name,
  in his legacy of good cheer,
  selfless service and integrity,
    in the lives of all he touched, changed and better because of
Mickey.

AT HIS MEMORIAL SERVICE, THIS WAS FRED'S PRAYER:

Mickey once said, "I am a Presbyterian – with Quaker tenden-cies."
Let us now honor those "Quaker tendencies" by praying in silence and quiet meditation. Let the spirit reach our souls.
· · · · · · ·
Lord, we remember Mickey –
we can see his smile and his bright eyes.
Lord, what a rich life –
teacher, writer, author, executive, volunteer, servant, witness,
prophet of justice, apostle of peace,
inveterate collector of tapes and articles, new ideas and old truths,
friend of the famous, champion of the outcasts –

always especially drawn to the underdogs, the
least of the brethren,
to those outside the camp, or inside the cage.
He knew how to win; he knew how to lose.
He knew what was more important than either.
He was a skilled administrator who never lost sight of persons –
who treated each one – whether Peewee Reese or peewee leaguer
with patience and care, gentleness and love.
Thank You, Lord, for his faith – sure and true and always growing.
Thank You, Lord for his deep conviction about putting faith into
practice,
justice into our imperfect world and mercy into
every relationship.
Unlike so many, he never demeaned, belittled,
put down others to assert himself,
but genuinely tried in daily obedience to his Lord
to follow Jesus into the prison walls
to meet and hear and help one prisoner – all prisoners,
to share bread with the starving
and to make peace in this warring world –
to bear Christ's yoke of love and hope
to all who were weary and heavy laden.

Be, O Lord… O be with Alice – welcome her tears,
receive her grief
strengthen her body and soul and uphold her faith.
Be with their sons now fatherless,
now bereft and mortal as never before –
and help them to honor their father and mother
by being the best, most authentic Donald and Michael they can
possibly be.
Be Lord, with all his family and all his friends in office or cell,
on the field, in the sanctuary
here and there and everywhere.

He always loved Your city, Lord, for he was an idealist and a dreamer,

an optimist, a man of faith.
We believe he lives there now – with Mr. Rickey, Jackie
and the cheering section of all the saints.
We remain in the human city emboldened to go on
to incarnate our faith
to follow his example
that every human city –
Brooklyn and Williamsport, Berkeley and Swannanoa
might be a more just, humane and loving place in which to live.
Amen.

Mickey McConnell

AL ROBERTS

THE REV. AL ROBERTS was the chaplain at the Farm School from 1934 till 1941, decades before Fred's tenure. He left for other notable pursuits within the ministry of the Presbyterian Church, but came back to work for the college in his retirement. He and his wife, Billie, built a house on College View Drive and lived there until their deaths.

OPENING WORDS AT HIS SERVICE IN 1976:

We come with relief and remorse
both joy and sorrow,
the heart resisting what the mind accepts,
the heart reaching past what the mind can know.
We come – and we are greeted by the company of friends
who care more than poor words can say.
We come – greeted by the bright memory of a good
and real man.
We come – greeted by the grace of God who is Love.

Let us free our hearts to faith and praise.

Fred then shared this reading:

There is a children's story – Margery Williams' *The Velveteen Rabbit* – that is one of those rare stories, like *The Little Prince*, which speaks to and touches the sensitivity of children and adults alike in its simplicity and its reality.

In a world of toys, new and shiny, used and discarded to be re-

placed by newer and shinier models —
in a world that identifies real with new,
beautiful with pretty
skin with soul
gadgetry with goodness
and pleasure with love,
the following simple conversation occurs between the Velveteen
Rabbit (no longer new) and the skin horse (old and worn and
wise):

"The Skin Horse knew all about being Real.

'What is REAL?' asked the Rabbit one day, 'Does it mean having things that buzz inside you and a stick-out handle?'

'Real isn't how you are made,' said the Skin Horse. 'When a
child loves you for a long, long time, not just to play with, but RE-
ALLY loves you, then you become Real.'

'Does it hurt?' asked the Rabbit.

'Sometimes,' said the Skin Horse. 'When you are Real you
don't mind being hurt.'

'Does it happen all at once,' he asked, 'like being wound up?'

'It doesn't happen all at once,' said the Skin Horse. 'By the
time you are Real, most of your hair has been loved off, and you get
very shabby. But once you are Real you can't become unreal again.
It lasts for always.'"

PRAYER:

Loving God, we come in faith
grateful that Al Roberts lived and died.

We remember his gifts to us and to so many others
who can't be here.
Who can measure, who can count all those he helped –
as an administrator – enabling, making possible change
and aid and love to so many who never knew him or met him?
He was a good and caring administrator –
in that maligned, necessary, and difficult ministry he did so well.
We each remember his gifts to us, as his kin, his friends,
his neighbors –
hear the silent appreciation of each one of us.

We bless You that he was a pastor –
O God, what a pastor to so many of us – able, patient, listening,
helpful.
Perhaps he had to learn, as do we,
that his ministry often went unappreciated,
that institutions don't love you,
people do.
They did and they do and they will.
Surely, he learned, as we are learning,
that the sharp edges are rubbed away –
by poverty, by candor, by hard work and pain and love.
How his body and soul were tested, his will tempted,
his soul purified
so that from the crucible of Your grace was fashioned
a hard-worn integrity,
a mellowness, a wholeness, that beautifully emerged.
Help us to join him – then – and now
in the breathtaking, awe-some process
of becoming more and more REAL.

Al Roberts

There are a few others who must be included in this book, although their files are incomplete:

VICTOR *and* CHRISTINA ELIASSEN

When we arrived at Warren Wilson in 1955 for Fred's internship from Yale, VICTOR and CHRISTINA ELIASSEN were living and working on the campus with their two young children. They were hard working, unusually talented and giving persons. Victor ran the print shop which was housed in an old structure where the Ogg Administration Building now stands. He was a very good artist, and his wood cuts were created for program covers, bulletins and were some of the college's first logos.

Meticulous in teaching his students the art of printing on the massive line-o-type machinery that produced all the materials needed by the college, he was highly respected for his craftsmanship. Any student with the slightest inclination toward the visual arts was put on the printing crew. They learned a great deal from their Mr. Eliassen, who was a shy, intelligent man with much to offer.

An unimaginable amount of work was turned out from that shop. He was a careful proofreader. What a skill that is. It was rare to find an error in any of his work. When the building was torn down, the whole printing operation was replaced by one small piece of "updated" machinery on the first floor of the Ad Building with Elena Law in charge. Victor's skills were dearly missed — especially by Miss Law!

Christina was a fine musician and Fred's first organist. She played for all the services and accompanied the choir and every musician ever to grace the stage in the Elizabeth Williams Chapel. Her volunteer work knew no limits – working so many hours for the Girl Scouts, receiving the highest honor given in scouting, volunteering with the PTA, Swannanoa Valley Inter-church Association, and holding many offices in the church.

At her memorial service, Fred praised her courage, saying, "I shall never forget this recent Holy Week last month, when Christina, knowing what must come, in great pain, played for the Communion Service, the Good Friday Service and Easter. She would not quit. She told me when she first knew that her time here was short, that she wanted to go on as long as God would let her." *I note that her death was in April 1959, and I remember it being a difficult and painful cancer. Her children were on the threshold of their teens and left motherless. It was one of the saddest times in my memory.*

Victor Eliassen is remembered by his student, **Milton Ohlsen,** *in these words:*

"Victor Eliassen was my 'boss,' and I say that almost reverently. He ran the print shop. We supplied the church bulletins, stationary, campus paper, and a host of other items. We (five of us) set the type by hand, ran the presses and did what we were capable of doing. The linotype was Mr. Eliassen's baby, and he was a pro.

The Heidelberg Press was the newest and best press we had. And, in some ways, it was the most dangerous because of the speed of its arms that grabbed the paper, took it to the platen and then, after printing, stacked it up. Boss thought it could hurt us, so there was strict oversight. What an honor to be allowed to run it.

That summer, because of my work at WWC, I procured a job in Asheville in a print shop. That allowed me the chance to continue my education at what is now Muskingum University, where I also worked part time in a print shop and kept off the indigent rolls. I think Mr. Eliassen would have been proud.

I never remember him raising his voice – and there were times when it was surprising that he did not. There were many Friday or Saturday nights when he worked quite late on his own so that the job would get done – especially the church bulletin. Never asked for help.

He would whistle softly to himself, and the print shop was always a quiet place so that we would hear him. That was my introduction to the classics. I liked to hear him whistle. He sounded happy.

Boss went to St. Olaf's College. Where, what, was that? While he did not share any information on that, I can report that whenever I heard/hear St. Olaf's mentioned, I remember him.

Somewhere along the way his head bent down and decided to stay that way. Never knew why. His pate was shiny. His walk was purposeful and strong, even fast. He was a private man to be sure, but one whom we admired, even loved. One of our crew wrote an article about him that was printed in the newspaper, *The Echo* or *The Owl and Spade* as a thank you to this gentle, humble, intelligent man.

I do not know this, but I think he was almost invisible on campus. If that were so, a lot of students and faculty were the poorer. He was a man of letters (pun intended) who to us was a gentleman and a scholar, who treated us with such kindness and gentleness that he earned our devotion and admiration."

Victor Eliassen did not live in the area when he died in 1977.

Victor Eliassen

Christina Eliassen

CYRUS *and* MARIAN ANDERSON

The ANDERSONS, both having had distinguished careers in the Navy, came to us in the 1960s with their four almost-grown children and countless animals. Dr. Anderson – ANDY – was hired to head the department of education, and we were so lucky to get him – and Marian along with him. I do not have Andy's memorial service because he died a very old man back in Florida with his children, but I must include them in this book because they were such a vital and important part of the college community.

MARIAN had one of the most unusual deaths, and I recount it often. It was a wonderful summer vacation day in France, with their daughter's family sitting happily outdoors at lunch. Marian reached over and asked her beloved granddaughter, "Emily, are you going to eat that olive?" and died. Just like that. The French doctor said, "Her heart just broke." (Ours too). As Fred said in her memorial service: There's no cure for a broken heart except for good faith, God's love, dear friends and great memories.

The campus, of course, was shocked when news reached us in July of 1995.

At her service, Fred quoted her daughter, **Suellen Hudson***: "No veterinarian ever cared more for animals or treated them with more respect, tenderness and love than she did."*

241

FRED'S WORDS AT MARIAN'S SERVICE:

I can still remember the first Sunday that Marian and Andy were in church, 26 years ago. We had one of our crazy services in which we played music from Dr. Doolittle, danced, talked to the animals and celebrated God's great ark. Bev and I couldn't help but wonder (and worry) what the newly arrived Andersons might think of it all. I got the most delightful and appreciative letter from Marian that week, in which she said that, as a friend of all God's creatures, she felt at home here. She was at home and her home reached out to include us all.

PRAYER:

We remember her adventurous spirit, her thirst for learning... and always asking what she could do to help.
Unlike some, she was always willing to do unheralded things, to clean up messes, to work without a spotlight.
Lord, she once said she didn't have any talents – No talent?!
...except for: her winsome optimism
her great good cheer
her beauty in and out
her verve
her graciousness
her irreverent, earthy, funny sense of humor, like when she described getting old as "pigeon poop," and said she would have none of it –
and she never got old, even at 81.
What a talent she had for loving all creatures, great or small, feral or tame. She nursed them, fed them, loved them, and paid You the great compliment of enjoying them, as she enjoyed Godiva chocolates and barbeque ribs, the delight of friendship and the enjoyment of EVERYthing...
or as her friend, Margi, put it,
"her sweet brown eyes drank in life..."

*   *   *   *   *

I must add a bit about her participation in the theater. Marian loved being a part of a cast and always came to audition for "just a little part." We often needed an older person, and she was cast many times. I dressed her in a plethora of strange costumes over the years, and she wore everything with such delight, even blackening her teeth as one of the witches in Macbeth. Festivals were when she shone brightest, taking part in every one, always willing and wanting to do more. You could always call on Andy or Marian for anything in the church or college and know it would be done well and with enthusiasm.

Andy chose well when he found Marian, and he was a smart one to know how much he needed her in his life. He loved her passionately and knew how much delightful spice there would be around him because of her. He always smiled and appeared to enjoy everything she did, and to quote **Betty Siviter***, retired head of the Early Learning Center, "Andy would do anything to make Marian happy." And happily ever after, they traveled extensively – far and wide, especially after Andy retired.*

Our Dr. Anderson was very competent, a dedicated educator, a very good man and a devoted, loving father. He did his work meticulously well and created a respected education department which produced decades of great teachers. They are all around us now, still receiving honors. The school administrators in many vicinities knew that if they got a WWC grad in education, they were getting a very special teacher. With his Navy background, Andy ran a tight and esteemed "ship."

Long after he retired he was still teaching courses for the department, and every time a new director would leave, there Andy would be taking over again, and heading the search until a new person was found. He was an expert in the intricacies of public school education, and his interest in educational psychology helped to make that department one of the best in the region.

Dean Kahl *recalls the Andersons in these words:*

"The Andersons were like grandparents to our daughters, Julie and Susie. In fact we called them 'Grandma Marian' and 'Poppy Andy.' We were often invited to their home for celebrations, like the Fourth of July.

Their kitchen was a warm and welcoming place with lots of good food, support and laughter. They helped to make Warren Wilson a true community. When our family had a health crisis, the Andersons often pitched in to look after our children or to transport family members to and from the hospital.

It was fun to talk to Andy about the Cincinnati Reds. He was a serious fan and liked to listen to their games on the radio. He suffered greatly as they often disappointed him."

Baseball was indeed Andy's other love, and what a supporting fan he was of the Asheville Tourists, going to as many games with his campus buddies as time would allow. His idea of a great evening was watching a game and having a hot dog for supper. His interest in sports took him over to our own athletic department at Warren Wilson, where he was welcomed, became Director of Athletics, where he worked tirelessly for all our teams and programs for many years.

Andy and Marian both held church offices and were active in every part of campus life − dearly cherished members of the community.

Andy and Marian Anderson

ELENA LAW

ELENA LAW just died the year this is being written, 2010, in LaJolla, California. She would have been 100 years old on a soon-to-be birthday. There were so many hard workers at Warren Wilson in those early days, but I dare say no one ever worked harder than Elena. If anyone, including administrators and faculty, ever needed to know anything about the college, its inhabitants, its function, its history, its ANYTHING, they would go to Elena and get the correct answer. She was never a gossip; she was just well informed. Not that we had Google then, but we would not have needed it with Elena around.

Her workspace was the first floor of the Ad Building, and we always said she ran the college. Her workload was enormous, especially after taking over the duties of the print shop. The light on the first floor of the Ad Building was often on until the wee hours of the morning. I think they called her the college secretary, but she was so much more than that. Everything she did was done well, so she kept getting more and more to do.

In addition to her official duties, she was everyone's travel agent. It was a hobby of hers to know the correct routes to everywhere, including air and train connections, so of course anyone making a trip would seek out Elena, and she would graciously help.

I recall once when she printed a festival booklet and everything was running late. It was done hastily by a student, and the pages were reversed, not in the right order. It was a huge festival celebrating HERITAGE and it was to begin the next day. That night, the Ad Building light stayed on until dawn, when unbeknownst to anyone, she re-cut and stapled hundreds of booklets herself so they could be handed out at the first event.

In earlier years, she was the one who opened the many packages that arrived through the mail from churches and "do-gooders." They usually came from northern locations and sent to help the "less fortunate" Appalachian students. Elena decided what was appropriate for the students and what was not. The theater received from those "mission barrels" many tuxedoes and fancy dresses (long out of style), sent by families of deceased ministers and their wives. We wondered if they really thought our students would wear such things, but the costume shop got some great period garments.

Reva Watson Dietrich, *who worked with Elena when she was a student in the early 1950's, remembers the time Elena fell and broke both her arms. She took only a few days off from her work and then came back and continued to work with both arms in casts. Talk about a work ethic.*

Maryam Daftari *remembers her fondly, and recently shared this: "Miss Law was such a gracious, gentle, kind, compassionate human being. With her lovely unusual grayish/white hair, she was always a picture of what a very moral and upright human being should be like. Always there to give a helping hand. I think of her still."*

Fred worked closely with Elena in the church and in the college. I can't recall how many offices she held, but there were many. This was a truly remarkable woman. When she retired early, we did think the college would cease, not able to function without her. When she moved to California, she continued to volunteer for presbytery and synod offices of the Presbyterian Church. How lucky they were.

I know that Fred would love to have done her memorial service. I wish he were here to say in his beautiful voice, "We are here today to honor and celebrate the life of Elena Law, beloved by us all..."

Fred did, however, make the presentation when she was honored on the occasion of her 25 years of service to Warren Wilson:

I've been asked to present a certificate from the board to recognize Elena Law. Now we all know this is not really correct. Elena Law's 25 years of overtime and nighttime and weekend work would, I reckon, work out to be anybody else's 50 years.

On behalf of your friends here, Elena, I'd like to add a few words to what the board has written.

Thank you...

— for all the letters, forms, bulletins, tests, papers, that even when handed in to you a day late came out on time, accurately, well done;

— for not only being able to actually understand plane and train and bus schedules, but also running the best travel agency in these or any parts;

— for providing maps and tax forms, for knowing the best route to anyplace, the best motels and restaurants anywhere;

— for somehow always being able to locate lost, strayed, misplaced papers, furniture, visitors and staff members;

— for being such an able secretary to the college, for being the kind of person we all turn to so often, day in and day out... when in doubt, ask Elena;

— and for doing all these things (and so many more) with integrity, gentleness, patience and humility.

It may well be that by grace we are saved — but at Warren Wilson, Law really helps.

Thank you, Elena.

Elena Law

POSTSCRIPT

It has been such a pleasure for me compiling these pages and adding to them. I revisited old and cherished friends who were a major part of my life. I was made aware once again what a remarkable group of people they were, as the memories of them flooded my mind. How very lucky I was to be a part of this community that is Warren Wilson College for so many years of its growth. I treasure it all and all of them.

When we were losing so many of these amazing people as they aged, the memorial services occurred much too often, and the tears attested to how much they were loved — truly loved. I would usually meet the Laursens leaving the chapel, and Pat and I always had a handkerchief in our hands and our red eyes matched. "How many more?" we would think. It truly was like losing our family.

Many of these saints are buried in the Warren Wilson Cemetery, located off Riceville Road on Dillingham Circle — a secluded, peaceful part of our college overlooking the mountains and pastures. It's holy ground and a spiritual place to visit.

As I write this, I have been working on the campus longer than any other person — first 18 years as a volunteer, then 32 years "officially."

What a privilege it has been.

ABOUT THE AUTHORS

Frederick Ohler was chaplain of Warren Wilson College, pastor of the Warren Wilson Presbyterian Church and College Chapel, counselor, teacher of religion, philosophy, and other related courses for almost 40 years. Beverly Ohler's life, in addition to the chapel, has always centered around the Warren Wilson theater, teaching and designing, producing festivals, creating art in one form or another.

Bev and Fred both grew up in Northern New Jersey, the New York City area, with sojourns to New Haven, Connecticut and northern California. Most of their life has been spent on the campus of Warren Wilson, where Bev shared Fred's ministry, where they raised their two daughters, Chrisann and Lisa, and where Bev is still part of the theater department. Fred died in January 2004.

The trustees of Warren Wilson College, at the request of hundreds of alumni, are naming the chapel and surrounding buildings – THE OHLER SPIRITUAL CENTER. A service scholarship is being established in Fred's name, to be given to a WWC student whose focus is to help others. All proceeds from this book will go toward the scholarship fund.

Fred and Bev Ohler
At the 1982 service celebrating 25 years at Warren Wilson

BENEDICTION

Founders' Day Celebration
November 21, 1994

A celebration lasts for an hour;
a century lasts for 36,525 days;
artifacts endure for centuries
and bones for millennia…
but influence goes on forever.

Who can imagine the next century –
two lifetimes,
a thousand fads,
and a million changes from now?

But know this: there will still and all-ways be
truth to learn,
work to do,
people to serve,
and God to love.
You get no guarantees…
only the promise of adventure,
the prospect of wonder,
and the company of God's providence.

God bless you, Warren Wilson College,
and all your daughters and sons.
Amen.

– Frederick Ohler

ALMA MATER

Where the stalwart pioneers
built their highland homes,
still our college presses near,
frontiers yet unknown.
Gold of sun across the sky,
cast of mountain blue,
glorious banner, heaven high
calls us to be true.
Take your place and do with us what tomorrow needs of you.

When the shadows sweep the light
from the face of day,
songs of freedom break the night. This is what they say:
God who raised our hills of home,
guard our fortress still,
walk with us along the way,
teach us wisdom till
like a thousand starts by night
we shall faithfully lead the way.

– Henry Jensen